DESIGNING TRAINING PROGRAMMES

Designing training programmes

Dick Leatherman

Gower

First published 1990 by Human Resource Development Press Inc.
This edition published by
Gower Publishing Limited
Gower House
Croft Road
Aldershot
Hampshire GU11 3HR
England

British Library Cataloguing in Publication Data
Leatherman, Dick
Designing training programmes
1. Employees – Training of   2. Executives – Training of
3. In-services training
I. Title
658.3'12404

ISBN 0 566 07770 1

Typeset in Linotype Palatino by Poole Typesetting (Wessex) Ltd, and printed in Great Britain at the University Press, Cambridge

Contents

List of figures

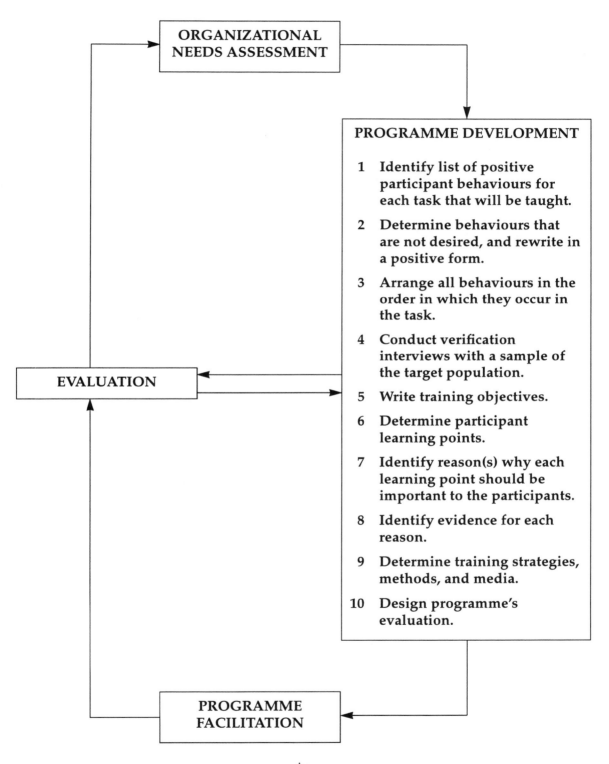

ORGANIZATIONAL
NEEDS ASSESSMENT

PROGRAMME DEVELOPMENT

1   Identify list of positive
    participant behaviours for
    each task that will be taught.

2   Determine behaviours that
    are not desired, and rewrite in
    a positive form.

3   Arrange all behaviours in the
    order in which they occur in
    the task.

4   Conduct verification
    interviews with a sample of
    the target population.

5   Write training objectives.

6   Determine participant
    learning points.

7   Identify reason(s) why each
    learning point should be
    important to the participants.

8   Identify evidence for each
    reason.

9   Determine training strategies,
    methods, and media.

10 Design programme's
    evaluation.

EVALUATION

PROGRAMME
FACILITATION

Designing Effective Training Programmes

Designing effective training programmes

Let us assume that you have already conducted a reliable needs assessment. As a result of this assessment, you have a specific list of programme topics needed by your target population. But before you begin your training programme, you need to examine carefully two key questions. First, how do you determine the content of a particular programme that you wish to teach? And second, how do you select the best teaching processes for that content? In order to help you make these critical decisions, we will first present a set of training design principles, and then a step-by-step method of programme development.

Learning principles

Good training design incorporates the following principles. It:

1 **Is based on an assessment of TRAINING needs.**
   Training is conducted to teach people what they don't know or can't do – not to teach people what they already know or can already do!
2 **Provides the participants with a variety of learning experiences.**
   There should be a mix of media (i.e., some video, some overhead transparencies and flip charts), and a mix in teaching strategies (i.e., lecture, subgroup work, general discussions, reading and role play).

In short, your training programme should be designed so that it is exciting and interesting to your participants.

3   **Involves the participants in the learning.**

Training strategies such as subgroup work, determining the participants' expectations and reservations, encouraging participants to offer their ideas and opinions, ensuring that some of the participants in the programme were included in the needs assessment and using pre-tests and post-tests are all ways you can involve your participants in their own learning.

4   **Reduces the tension felt by the participants.**

Presenting topic outlines and objectives at the beginning of the programme, allowing time for introductions and/or 'ice-breakers', conducting role plays in a non-threatening manner, avoiding calling on specific participants by name to provide the answers to questions and using subgroup work to allow participants to provide anonymous answers to difficult questions are some of the many things you can do to keep participants from becoming anxious.

5   **Is relevant to the participants' 'real world'.**

Training programmes can be designed to relate to what the participants do for a living by:
- making sure that a needs assessment is conducted
- using 'cases' that are realistic
- selecting videotapes that portray environments that are similar to those the participants work in.

6   **Results in programmes that relate to the participants' experiences.**

If I find out what my participants already know, I can use this information to teach new concepts. For example, when I was a teenager, I was taught the Pythagorean theorem. I memorized it and could use it. But I was 49 years old before I really understood it.

A remarkable ex-Navy instructor was teaching an adult electronics class, and I saw him present the theorem as follows:

> 'Now', he asked his class, 'does anyone remember the Pythagorean theorem?' 'Sure', one class member replied, 'Side A squared plus side B squared is equal to the hypotenuse squared.' 'Outstanding!' the instructor replied. 'But what does that mean?' There was total silence. He then picked up a piece of chalk and drew the diagram shown in Figure 1.
>
> Then he asked, 'How do you determine the area of a square?' Several students responded by saying that you simply multiply one side by itself. 'Correct!' he said. 'What the Pythagorean theorem actually means is that if you have two squares whose sides form the two legs of a right triangle (sides a and b), then the area of these two squares is equal to the area of the square formed by the triangle's third side (hypotenuse).'

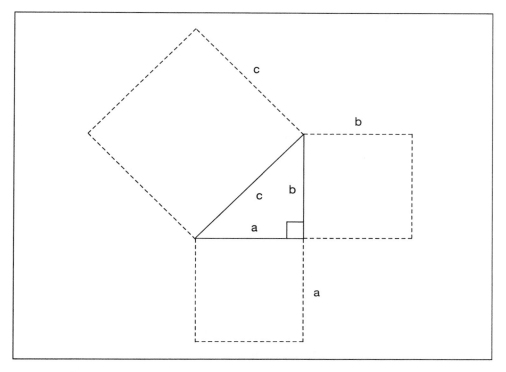

Figure 1   Pythagoras' theorem

At this point, his group had a solid understanding of the Pythagorean theorem, and would probably remember it forever. He found out what they already knew (area of a square) and related it to the new knowledge (Pythagoras' theorem). Good teachers and trainers have a way of taking complex things and making them simple by building new information on old knowledge.

This principle of effective training can be designed into your programmes during the planning stage by: 1) planning for enough time so that you can ask questions to find out what the group already knows about a specific topic; 2) doing a thorough needs assessment that determines what the participants already know; and 3) devoting enough time to subgroup work for the participants to have a real opportunity to utilize their prior knowledge.

7 **Takes into account the fact that participants tend to remember best what they both see and hear, versus what they are only told.**
Use transparencies and prepared flip charts; or if neither of these two media are available, use the blackboard.

8   **Provides the participants with an opportunity to DO what it is they are being taught.**

Here is a tongue-in-cheek example of illustrating how important this principle is. Suppose that I had a lifelong ambition to be a medical doctor. But unfortunately, my dream was never realized. One day, while reading a *Popular Mechanics* magazine, I saw a classified ad that said, 'Make big bucks!!! Learn to be a physician at home on your own time through our approved correspondence training program!'

So I signed up, sent in my cheque, and began receiving my reading asignments. As it turned out, I was pretty good at learning the material, and made high grades on all my open-book exams. I found the section on 'Removing the Appendix' especially fascinating, and as a result made an A+ on that particular lesson.

Now the question is, how would you feel about me taking out YOUR appendix? But we too often ask participants to 'take out an appendix' when all they have been provided is information, with no skill practice.

This principle simply means that if you want your participants to be able to *do* something after the training is over, then don't just 'tell' them how. Give them a chance to do it!

9   **Uses repetition to help the participants learn.**

Tell your participants what you are going to teach them. Then explain it, demonstrate it, have them do it themselves – and then discuss what they did. Or you can use transparencies to present the topic, and then have them read about it in your handouts. Also use summaries throughout the training programme to reinforce what has already been discussed. If the programme covers several days, recap what was covered the previous day before starting on new material.

10   **Focuses on QUALITY of instruction, not quantity!**

Quality training begins with an effective needs assessment, and continues to quality design. Unfortunately, we are often pulled in two directions at once: we have much content to cover, but a very limited amount of training time with the participants. The tendency is to squeeze in as much material as we can through 'telling', while reducing the quality of the training programme by omitting discussion, subgroup workshops, role play and other important learning experiences. Remember that your original objective is to provide quality training that really makes a difference. And quality training takes a lot of time – both time spent in planning sound training strategies and time in the classroom.

11   **Provides for following up on the job what has been taught in the classroom.**

There are a number of things that you can do to provide follow-up help for the participants. For example, you can train the bosses of the participants to provide job reinforcement on what is taught in training. Or you can include a commitment exercise at the end of the training programme in which the participants publicly state what they plan to do differently and better on the job with what they have learned. You can schedule personal follow-up visits with each of the participants. And even something as simple as providing detailed handouts of the programme's content can help the participants apply on the job what they have learned in the classroom.

12 **Includes evaluation as a part of the original planning process.**
The time to determine how you are going to evaluate a programme is when you are designing the programme – not after the programme is completed.

Programme planning process: An overview

We can use the principles above to help us make better decisions about programme content, training strategies and training media. Each step in the planning process that follows should be approached with these principles in mind.

In the discussion and examples that follow, we have selected leaders as our target audience and 'Leadership' as the content to be taught. We will use this group and topic because it is often one of the major training responsibilities of an in-house trainer. But the planning process works equally well for sales training, technical training and even in developing programmes for colleges and universities.

We will use the word 'leader' to describe anyone who may be in a leadership position. We have avoided the use of words like 'supervisor' or 'manager' since they are unduly restrictive. In fact, a leader might be an executive or even an employee who has some leadership responsibility.

We can design a training programme by using the following ten-step planning process:

1 **Make a list of positive participant behaviours for each task that will be taught.**
Example: If the task is 'Delegation', then one of the many behaviours that could be listed – and later taught to the participants – is, 'Select the appropriate person to perform a delegated job'.

2 **Identify undesirable participant behaviours, and rewrite them in positive form.**
Example: If the task is 'Delegation', then a negative behaviour might

be 'Not delegating work due to fear of losing control'. This behaviour can be rewritten as a positive behaviour thus: 'Delegating work without fear of losing control'.

3   **Order the final list of all behaviours.**
Arrange all of the behaviours in the order in which they normally occur as the task is carried out, including the behaviours from both step 1 and step 2.

4   **Conduct verification interviews with a sample of the target population to determine which task behaviours are being performed well, and which are not.**
Example: Interview members of the target population to determine why some individuals are not delegating work. If the majority in this group are comfortable giving up part of their responsibilities (i.e., delegating), without feeling that they would be 'losing control', then it will not be necessary to spend future training time on this particular behaviour.

5   **Write training objectives.**
Example: If the task is 'Delegation', and one of the behaviours is, 'Select the appropriate person to perform a delegated job', then rewrite this behaviour as an objective: 'Given a decision making matrix and delegation criteria, the participant will be able to select the appropriate person for a delegated job.'

6   **Determine required participant learning points for each objective.**
Example: Again using the objective in step 5, the participant might need to know how to:
  - identify tasks that can be delegated
  - identify tasks that cannot be delegated
  - analyse the tasks to be delegated, determining specific activities required to complete each task
  - analyse employees' workloads, and determine which employees have available time.

7   **Identify participant reasons why the knowledge and skills are important.**
Example: Continuing the example in step 6 above, you might indicate the following reason as to why it is important to 'identify tasks that can be delegated': 'You need to write out and then evaluate the things you actually do in your job since there is a strong likelihood you will find something that you could have delegated but didn't because you LIKED doing that thing.'

8   **Identify evidence (examples, analogies, and/or authorities) for each of the reasons listed in step 7.**
Example: – Louis Allen's research showing that most leaders could delegate more of their work – but don't!

– Personal anecdote telling how I open all my mail (which is 90 per cent junk mail) myself because I like opening my mail – even though it is a simple job that could easily be delegated.

9   Determine training strategies, methods and media.

Example: 1   Present the key point that most of us have things we do that could be delegated.

2   Highlight Louis Allen's research using overhead transparency.

3   Pass out worksheet titled, 'Delegation Worksheet'.

4   Ask participants to individually list their job tasks on the worksheet, and then determine if there are any items that could be delegated but haven't been because they enjoy doing them.

5   Ask if anyone can give a personal example.

6   Etc.

10   Design the programme's evaluation.

Example: Since delegation will take place on the job, you decide to construct an on-the-job evaluation to be done three months after the programme is completed.

Utilizing the ten-step model outlined above, suppose you send out to all of your leaders a needs assessment instrument which clearly reveals that the great majority of them are not comfortable conducting performance appraisals with their people. In addition, the personnel department has completed an attitude survey of all employees, and has found strong, negative feelings about performance appraisals.

Now also suppose you know that the difficulty is not due to a poor performance appraisal system (the forms that were used by the leaders were excellent, and the paperwork flow was appropriate).

At this point, you need to know what is involved in an effective performance appraisal interview before attempting to find out what your leaders are actually doing when they conduct their interviews. In other words, first determine the key things (behaviours) a leader does when conducting an effective performance appraisal interview, and *then* attempt to verify what is really going on with your leaders. You can specify what should be happening by researching the job itself, and listing those things that an effective leader does in conducting a performance appraisal interview.

After you determine what your leaders are actually doing, then delete any items on your original behaviour list which they are already doing, and thus don't need to learn. Then rewrite the remaining items in the form of training objectives, and identify the knowledge and skills (learning points) which the leaders will need in order to implement each of the objectives that is on your final list. Next, list the reasons why the knowledge and skills represent appropriate leader behaviour. Then, identify examples, analogies and/or authorities, and select the appropriate training strategies and media to teach the content. Finally, because performance appraisal interviews are normally conducted in private, select an evaluation strategy that will allow you to evaluate the participant's behaviour at the close of the programme, rather than on the job.

This may seem like a lot of work. And it is! But this upfront, intensive planning can result in remarkable training sessions that will yield positive results for the organization, the participants and you.

Step 1 – Positive participant behaviours

The first step in programme planning is to develop a list of behaviours which together cover all of the important things that should be done in the task that is being analysed. Using this approach, Elton Mayo of the Harvard Graduate School and G.A. Pennock at Western Electric began research in 1927 which later became the classic five-year Hawthorne study. From this study came a four-step leadership model which listed the following tasks:

1   Get the facts.
2   Weigh and decide.
3   Take action.
4   Check results.

Today this model seems very simplistic. At the time, however, it constituted a major breakthrough in that it was the first formalization of leadership behaviours.

In the years that have followed, a great deal of research has been conducted on leadership behaviour, and we are now able to identify key behaviours required in a wide variety of management situations. For example, from the work of Charles Kepner and Benjamin Tregoe we can identify the specific leadership behaviours required to teach decision-making and problem-solving. Similarly, David McClelland's research on 'need achievement' has enabled us to determine the specific behaviours used by leaders in setting goals and objectives with their employees.

When you are preparing to teach a specific topic (a series of tasks) to future participants, there are a number of places you can look for the relevant behaviours to be taught. First, you might select appropriate journal articles and books to assist you in developing your list of task behaviours.

Secondly, subject-matter experts can likewise assist you in developing lists of key task behaviours. Such experts might be the authors of specific books or journal articles covering the topic that you will be presenting. Training seminars and conferences feature hundreds of quality speakers on nearly every human resource topic. And almost without exception, speakers and authors will be extremely gracious in sharing their experience and advice.

Imagine now that we are actually going to develop a performance appraisal programme to teach our leaders how to conduct effective interviews. After careful analysis of a number of professional articles and books, and securing suggestions from subject-matter experts, we might arrive at the following list of behaviours:

PROGRAMME DEVELOPMENT WORKSHEETS
(Page 1 of 5 pages)

1   POSITIVE PARTICIPANT BEHAVIOURS
    TOPIC: Performance Appraisal Interviews
    REFERENCES:

Title of book or article	Author
Performance Appraisal and the Manager	Keil
What To Do About Performance Appraisal	Kellogg
Appraising Managers as Managers	Koontz
The Supervisor's Complete Guide to Leadership Behaviour	Leatherman
Effective Motivation Through Performance Appraisal	Lefton
The Appraisal Interview	Maier
Win-Win Performance Management Appraisal	Rausch

POSITIVE BEHAVIOURS (not necessarily in order at this time):
– Discuss an employee's ratings in a non-threatening way.
– Bring up areas of concern about the employee's performance.
– Help the employee analyse the cause of any performance problems.
– Probe for employee solutions to any problems discussed.
– Use words or phrases that aren't judgemental.
– Put the employee at ease.
– Prepare an employee for a performance appraisal session.
– Complete the detailed preparation necessary to ensure a good performance appraisal discussion.
– Ask questions to enlist an employee's early involvement in the session.
– Develop written action plans with an employee.

- Provide positive feedback to an employee on the employee's strengths.
- Set follow-up dates.
- Summarize the interview.

© ITC, Inc.

Step 2 – Identify undesirable participant behaviours and rewrite in positive form

It is not only important to determine the things that should be done in the task that will be taught, but also to look at the behaviours that are *not* appropriate. This is particularly important in that by examining undesirable (or negative) behaviours closely, we may see additional positive behaviours that we have overlooked. Note that these are *not* just the earlier positive behaviours written in negative form, but are new behaviours that should be avoided by the trainee.

The following example is a partial list of possible undesirable behaviours that we need to consider in designing our performance appraisal programme.

Note that each of the undesirable behaviours illustrated below can be reformulated as positive behaviours. For example, 'Interrupting the employee' can be rewritten as a positive behaviour, 'Avoid interrupting the employee'.

PROGRAMME DEVELOPMENT WORKSHEETS
(Page 2 of 5 pages)

2   IDENTIFY ANY UNDESIRABLE BEHAVIOURS:
- Interrupting the employee.
- Locating the performance appraisal meeting where privacy is not guaranteed.
- Allowing telephone calls or drop-in guests to interrupt the performance appraisal interview.
- Leader doing most of the talking.
- Having the performance appraisal form typed out in advance (it should be written in pencil).
- Not allowing enough time, causing the employee to feel pressured.

Now rewrite them in positive form:
- Avoid interrupting employee.
- Arrange meeting so that privacy is assured.

- Set up meeting to prevent interruptions.
- Encourage employee to do most of the talking.
- Prepare tentative performance appraisal form in pencil.
- Set aside a block of time so the interview can run over if needed.

© ITC, Inc.

Step 3 – Ordering the behaviours

The next step in our analysis is to write the positive behaviours from pages 3 and 2 on page 5 in the order in which they are actually performed. (The page 5 list, of course, now includes all of the negative behaviours from page 4, stated in positive terms.)

Our new – ordered – list follows:

PROGRAMME DEVELOPMENT WORKSHEETS
(Page 3 of 5 pages)

3   ORDER THE FINAL LIST OF ALL BEHAVIOURS IN THE WAY THAT THEY WOULD NATURALLY OCCUR WHEN PERFORMED IN A TASK – WITH THE NEGATIVE BEHAVIOURS REWRITTEN AND INCLUDED AS POSITIVE BEHAVIOURS:

- Complete the detailed preparation necessary to ensure a good performance appraisal discussion.
- Fill out the performance appraisal form in advance in pencil (not typed).
- Prepare an employee for a performance appraisal session.
- Arrange a private location for the interview.
- Ensure that the meeting is not interrupted.
- Set aside ample time for the interview.
- Put the employee at ease.
- Use words or phrases that aren't judgemental.
- Allow the employee to do most of the talking.
- Ask questions to enlist the employee's early involvement in the session.
- Bring up areas of concern about the employee's performance.
- Help the employee analyse the cause of any performance problems.
- Probe for employee solutions to any problems discussed.
- Develop written action plans with the employee.
- Provide positive feedback to the employee on the employee's strengths.

- Discuss the employee's ratings in a non-threatening way.
- Summarize the interview.
- Set follow-up dates.

© ITC, Inc.

Step 4 – Verification interviews

The next step in the ten-step process is to determine what our target audience is doing compared to our knowledge of what they should be doing, by conducting verification interviews. In our performance appraisal example, now that we have a good idea of what an effective interview looks like, we are in a much better position to verify what our leaders are actually doing. By interviewing a sample of our target population, we are now able to determine what the leaders are already doing well, and what they are not doing well – or at all.

A typical interview with a leader – named 'Bill' – might go as follows:

You: 'Tell me, Bill, what are your concerns about performance appraisals?'

Bill: 'I just wish the employees took them a little more seriously.'

You: 'Tell me more. What do you mean by "seriously"?'

Bill: 'I don't know exactly. They don't really participate. You know, they just sit there and listen – and I end up doing all the talking.'

You: 'So you wish that they would talk with you more during the interviews?'

Bill: 'Exactly!'

You: 'What do you do when you conduct an interview?'

Bill: 'Well, I spend a lot of time preparing for the sessions, reviewing past records, filling out the forms and so forth. Of course, my boss has to review the form and sign off on it.'

You: 'Then what?'

Bill: 'Then I schedule them for their interviews.'

You: 'Where do you hold the interviews?'

Bill: 'Here.'

You: 'What do you do about your phones, drop-in visitors, or – given these half-wall glass partitions – privacy?'

Bill: 'Well, I have to be available in case there is a problem. So when the phone rings, I just excuse myself for a minute and take care of the problem. As for the partitions, it is so noisy in here anyway that nobody else can hear what is going on.'

You: 'How much time do you schedule for each interview?'

Bill: 'Because my boss usually gets all of the interview forms to me at the last minute, I am under a lot of pressure to get the interview completed as quickly as possible, in order to be able to turn them in to the personnel department on time. So I try to schedule my 16 employees over a two-day period of time, which gives me plenty of time – maybe 30 to 40 minutes with each one.'

You: 'I see. What happens during the interview?'

Bill: 'I tell them what their strengths and weaknesses are. Then I show them what I have written on the form, and ask them if they have anything to add. If not, I get them to sign the form, showing that they have seen it.'

You: 'What kind of things do you get when you ask them for their comments?'

Bill: 'Not much. Oh, there are always a few who get upset about a particular rating. But usually they don't say much.'

You: 'I'm curious, Bill. What do you do to prepare the employees *before* the performance appraisal session?'

Bill: 'What do you mean?'

You: 'Do you spend any time with them prior to the session explaining how you will be conducting the interviews?'

Bill: 'No – because all of my people have been through these performance appraisal interviews with me before. So they know what to expect.'

You: 'Oh. Bill, you mentioned earlier that you tell your people what their strengths and weaknesses are. How do you do that?'

Bill: 'I just read what I wrote.'

You: 'Could you show me an example of a typical evaluation that you completed this past year?'

Bill: 'Sure, I keep copies of all the past appraisal forms. (Bill looks in a filing cabinet and pulls out a completed form.) Here's one.'

You: 'OK. I see you wrote as a strength, "Betty is extremely conscientious in the performance of her duties". What did you actually say to her?'

Bill: 'I guess that I said pretty much what I wrote.'

You: 'I see. Bill, you also described a weakness as, "Betty sometimes tends to be argumentative". What did you mean by that?'

Bill: 'She is! Sometimes when she gets an idea about how to do the job differently, even when the idea doesn't make sense, she won't drop it. Times like that she's a real pain!'

You: 'What did you tell her in the interview?'

Bill: 'Just what I wrote.'

You: 'OK Bill, just one last question. What kind of follow-up do you do after conducting the interviews?'

Bill: (Laughs.) 'Well, we conduct the appraisals again in one year.'

You: 'OK. I think I have enough for now. Thanks a lot for your time. You have been a great help in making whatever training we do on this subject meet your needs.'

Bill: 'No problem.'

Use the information gained from the preceding interview, and on the following page, examine the list of behaviours and indicate which are likely to require training, which will not require training (either because the leaders already know how to do them ,or training is NOT a solution) and which cannot be identified because of lack of information.

PROGRAMME DEVELOPMENT WORKSHEETS
(Page 3 of 5 pages)

3   ORDER THE FINAL LIST OF ALL BEHAVIOURS IN THE WAY THAT THEY WOULD NATURALLY OCCUR WHEN PERFORMED IN A TASK – WITH THE NEGATIVE BEHAVIOURS REWRITTEN AND INCLUDED AS POSITIVE BEHAVIOURS

4   VERIFICATION OF BEHAVIOURS THROUGH INTERVIEWS

Training needed = 'Yes'
Training not the solution = 'No'
Probably already know = 'R'
Unknown = 'U'

Complete the detailed preparation necessary to ensure a good performance appraisal discussion . . . . _____

Fill out the performance appraisal form in advance in pencil (not typed) . . . . _____

Prepare an employee for a performance appraisal session . _____

Arrange a private location for the interview . . . . _____

Ensure that the meeting is not interrupted . . . . _____

Set aside ample time for the interview . . . . _____

Put the employee at ease . . . . _____

Use words or phrases that aren't judgemental . . . . _____

Allow the employee to do most of the talking . . . . _____

Ask questions to enlist the employee's early involvement
in the session . . . .   _____
Bring up areas of concern about the employee's
performance . . . .   _____
Help the employee analyse the cause of any performance
problems . . . .   _____
Probe for employee solutions to any problems discussed . .   _____
Develop written action plans with the employee . . . .   _____
Provide positive feedback to the employee on the
employee's strengths . . . .   _____
Discuss the employee's ratings in a non-threatening way . .   _____
Summarize the interview . . . .   _____
Set follow-up dates . . . .   _____
© ITC, Inc.

We could continue with this particular verification interview, but you have probably already picked out some glaring needs. For example, this leader's performance appraisal interviews appear mainly to be 'presentations' on his part. And in addition, the leader needs to communicate to his employees his expectations about needed changes in the appraisal interview – *prior* to the meeting. You probably already noted that the second behaviour on the list (fill out the form in pencil) is NOT a training solution. That is, the system of having the managers 'sign off' on the form before the appraisal interview is conducted forces the leader to make a presentation to his people. In this case, the solution is to change the system, *not* do training.

We can now take the information we have learned in this verification interview and tentatively list some things we would like the leaders to do more effectively:

1   Meet with the employees in advance of the interview and discuss with them how the meeting will be handled differently than in the past.
2   Help the employees appraise themselves by filling out their own personal performance appraisal form in advance of the meeting.
3   During the interview, obtain more input from the employee.
4   Etc.

In this example, let us say that the leaders seemed to be highly motivated to do a good job, and expressed a strong desire to be 'fair' with their people when conducting performance appraisals. But most of the interviews which the leaders conducted were 'Sit-down, shut-up-and-listen,' one-way presentations, with little input from their employees. At this point, we realize that they would probably conduct better performance appraisal interviews, if they knew *how* to do so. In other words, 'they would if they could'. And since they could, but don't, they probably don't because they don't know how!

When you finish your interviews with a sample of the target population, you can look at your original list of behaviours and check off what they are already doing well and don't need to be taught. The behaviours that now remain on the list – those the leaders are not doing – are what need to be taught.

Assuming that we have found some behaviours that do not require training because the leaders were already performing well in these areas, let's continue the earlier example.

Step 5 – Training objectives

When we have identified through our verification interviews that our future participants lack specific knowledge or skills, then the solution is also clear: training. But before we begin designing the training programmes, we first have to ask ourselves what we want the participants to be able to do when they finish the training workshop. In other words, WHAT ARE THE TRAINING OBJECTIVES FOR OUR PARTICIPANTS?

A training objective is simply a statement of what we want the participants to be able to do when they have finished the training programme. In other words. What should they be able to do that they are not now doing? Thus a training objective is not what you as a trainer will do, but what your participants will be able to do after the training has been completed.

A strong payoff in using a behavioural analysis approach such as we have outlined here is that the list of behavioural statements we develop is easily rewritten as training objectives. Such statements help us to write specific and measurable training objectives which tell us – and the participants – what they should be able to do at the conclusion of the workshop. And in order to be useful, good training objectives have three characteristics:

1   Training objective statements should indicate *specific behaviours*. For example, the statement, 'Obtain more input from the employee' doesn't communicate enough information. How will I know when the participants have learned how to do this? Since the statement doesn't indicate clearly what the participants will DO when they complete the training, both the trainer and the participants will have a hard time knowing when they have successfully learned what was taught. Therefore, we can better write our original statement by either:
    – determining what the leaders will DO in order to obtain more input

from the employee (ask questions, listen without interrupting, start the interview by asking the employee for the topic he or she wishes to discuss first, etc.); or

  – identifying end results (e.g., increased employee acceptance of performance appraisal interviews as evidenced by a new attitude survey).

2 A training objective statement should also be as *quantifiable* as possible. For example, the statement above – 'increased employee acceptance of performance appraisal interviews as evidenced by a new attitude survey' – is not quantifiable as written. Therefore, we would have to accept ANY increase in employee acceptance as evidence that we have reached our objective.

Thus it may be necessary to specify what we mean by the word 'increased'. For example, we could define 'increase' as: 'The employee's average performance appraisal attitude scores wil be 25 per cent above the previous score, on a new survey.' The more we specify exactly what we mean when we write training objectives, the easier it will be to evaluate the training, and determine whether or not we have been successful.

3 Good training objectives should also be *achievable*. In other words, don't write objectives that set the participants and you up for failure. This often happens when conscientious trainers try to write too many objectives for the training time allowed.

PROGRAMME DEVELOPMENT WORKSHEETS
(Page 3 of 5 pages)

3 ORDER THE FINAL LIST OF ALL BEHAVIOURS IN THE WAY THAT THEY WOULD NATURALLY OCCUR WHEN PERFORMED IN A TASK – WITH THE NEGATIVE BEHAVIOURS REWRITTEN AND INCLUDED AS POSITIVE BEHAVIOURS

4 VERIFICATION OF BEHAVIOURS THROUGH INTERVIEWS

Training needed = 'Yes'
Training not the solution = 'No'
Probably already know = 'R'
Unknown = 'U'

Complete the detailed preparation necessary to ensure a good performance appraisal discussion ....Yes
Fill out the performance appraisal form in advance in pencil (not typed) ....No
Prepare an employee for a performance appraisal session ....Yes
Arrange a private location for the interview ....Yes
Ensure that the meeting is not interrupted ....Yes

Set aside ample time for the interview..Yes
Put the employee at ease...U
Use words or phrases that aren't judgemental ....Yes
Allow the employee to do most of the talking.......................................Yes
Ask questions to enlist the employee's early involvement
in the session ....Yes
Bring up areas of concern about the employee's
performance ....Yes
Help the employee analyse the cause of any performance
problems ....Yes
Probe for employee solutions to any problems discussed ....Yes
Develop written action plans with the employee.................................Yes
Provide positive feedback to the employee on the
employee's strengths..Yes
Discuss the employee's ratings in a non-threatening way......................U
Summarize the interview ....Yes
Set follow-up dates..Yes
© ITC, Inc.

After deleting the behaviours that do not need to be taught, we can now move on to the next step in our preparation – writing training objectives.

Returning to our previous performance appraisal example, we see that of the 18 total behaviours listed and verified, 15 were answered 'yes' – and are therefore needs requiring training. We would now write 15 training objectives for these listed behaviours.

As an illustration, we will show the first three objectives below:

PROGRAMME DEVELOPMENT WORKSHEETS
(Page 4 of 5 pages)

---

5   TRAINING OBJECTIVE WORKSHEET
(Write objectives on only those behaviours which the participants need to learn.)

Objective: A statement of what the participants are to be like when they
have successfully completed a learning experience.
– Observable behaviour   – Measurable behaviour
A. Identify specific behaviours that need to be taught.
B. Make the objectives quantifiable if possible.
C. Write objectives that are achievable.
1   The participants in the training programme will be able to
describe one key reason why the performance appraisal

form that is completed in advance of the meeting should not be typed, but filled out in pencil.

2   In a role play exercise with another participant in the training programme, the participant should be able to say to the employee, 'Here are the forms we will be using. Look them over, and if you have any questions, I'll be glad to answer them. I'd like you to fill out this form in advance of our interview. Examine your personal ideas about the job, and how well you're performing in each area. Consider any special problems or recommendations for discussion, and develop some specific plans for further improving your job performance.'

3   Given the past performance records of an actual employee who works for the participant, each participant in the training session will be able to list the employee's major strengths.

4   Etc.

© ITC, Inc.

In Lewis Carroll's *Alice in Wonderland*, Alice says to the Cheshire Cat, 'Would you tell me, please, which way I ought to go from here?' 'That depends a good deal on where you want to get to,' says the Cat. 'I don't much care where —' says Alice. 'Then it doesn't matter which way you go,' says the Cat.

If we don't know where we are going with our training, then it really doesn't make much difference what we do. But if we have very real objectives that must be accomplished, it makes a great deal of difference how we use our valuable training time.

Step 6 – Determining participant learning points for each objective

The sixth step in our ten-step process is to determine what the participants need to know and do in order for them to be able to complete a specific objective. If we can identify the specific information they need for each objective, then we will know exactly what should be taught in the training programme.

One good way for us to gather this information is to write each of our training objectives at the top of a sheet of paper. Then, with all the objectives in mind, review the literature used when we first determined the list of behaviours. In addition, specific objectives also allow us to look to other areas of knowledge for information on the topic being researched.

For example, if we are attempting to determine the knowledge and skills needed to discuss an area of concern with an employee in a performance appraisal interview, then we could also review the literature that deals with coaching as well as with problem-solving. Often when we are seeking knowledge about a specific objective in a training topic (such as performance appraisal), we can even look beyond the business world *per se*, examining research in fields like psychology or sociology.

If we track our performance appraisal example through to this next step, it might look something like this:

PROGRAMME DEVELOPMENT WORKSHEETS
(Page 5 of 5 pages)

Use a separate page for each objective that will be taught.
Objective 3: 'Given past performance records of an actual employee who works for the leader, each leader in the training session will be able to discuss the employee's strengths.'

---

6   DETERMINING REQUIRED PARTICIPANT LEARNING POINTS
List what the participant should know in order to achieve each objective. Discuss employee's strengths by describing their specific behaviours, and illustrating with examples; explain why it was important for the people involved; spell out future expectations; express appreciation; and develop action plans to utilize the employee's strengths if appropriate.
© ITC, Inc.

Step 7 – Identifying participant reasons why learning points are important

The next step in our planning process is to identify the individual reasons for each learning point necessary to complete the objective. When we teach specific content to our participants, they need to know the underlying reasons why they should do what we are asking them to do. For example, if one of our learning points is, 'Allow the employee to do most of the talking', then we need to be able to present the reasons why this is important.

Participants can be required to do certain things in a workshop, and for whatever reasons they will do them – to get us off their backs, peer pressure due to everyone else in the group doing it, etc. But if we want to ensure that they will actually do outside of the classroom what they are being taught to do, then we need to communicate clearly the common-sense reasons why the behaviours are important. In other words, they must believe in the value of what they are being taught. Therefore, as we research our initial list of behaviours, we also need to make notes on the rationale for each behavioural learning point.

Take the following example. Suppose that one of our learning points is, 'Allow the employees to do most of the talking.' This might be a significant departure from the way in which our leaders have conducted performance appraisals in the past. The leaders may have viewed a performance appraisal 'presentation' as a quick and easy process. And since the employee's interaction was minimal, arguments were kept to a minimum.

With these preconceived reasons for continuing to do appraisals the way they have always been done, the leaders in our training programme will need clear and powerful reasons for changing their behaviours. Therefore, as we do our initial research, we need to identify the reasons for recommended behaviours. In this example, we may discover that there are powerful reasons why it's important to encourage the employee to do most of the talking.

Continuing with our earlier example – i.e., leaders who need training in performance appraisal – the following is an example of step 7.

PROGRAMME DEVELOPMENT WORKSHEETS
(Page 5 of 5 pages)

Use a separate page for each objective that will be taught.
5   Objective 3: 'Given past performance records of an actual employee who works for the leader, each leader in the training session will be able to discuss the employee's strengths.'

---

6   DETERMINING REQUIRED PARTICIPANT LEARNING POINTS
    List what the participants should know in order to achieve each objective. A) 'Leaders need to discuss employee's strengths in a performance appraisal interview. This is accomplished by: B) describing their specific behaviours, and illustrating with examples; C) explaining why it was important for the people involved; D) spelling out future expectations; E) expressing appreciation; and F) developing action plans to utilize the employee's strengths if appropriate.'

7 IDENTIFY REASONS FOR EACH ACKNOWLEDGED ITEM AND SKILL

List the learning points and give reasons why EACH represents appropriate participant behaviour.

1 Leaders need to discuss employee's positive performance in a performance appraisal session.	– Employees need to know what their leader perceives as important. – Employees tend to continue doing what they are reinforced for doing. – Increases the employee's morale because most people enjoy being honestly recognized for what they do. – Increases production.
2 Discuss employee's strengths by describing specific behaviours, illustrating with examples.	– Makes the statements believable, i.e., the employee realizes that the leader really does know exactly what the employee's positive performances were.
3 Etc.	

© ITC, Inc.

For each knowledge unit and skill, we list the key reasons why it is important. And these are the reasons that need to be communicated to our future participants during our training programme.

Step 8 – Identifying evidence

In order to make the reasons offered in step 7 more acceptable – and more believable – to your participants, offer sound evidence or proof to support your statements. Since most evidence is presented in terms of what the participants already know, it also helps them to learn new information if you relate it to their past experience. Here are some forms evidence can take:

1 **An incident**. This is often referred to as 'analogy' – a story which supports one's argument by demonstrating the point in a different context.

Example:
When teaching participants the need to listen, I often tell them about the time I was talking to an agronomist (a clever farmer) in Williamsburg, Virginia. The visit had nothing to do with 'training'.

But I was doing what I tend to do too much of – talking! And while I talked, this 75-year-old gentleman listened. I kept on talking and he kept on listening. Finally, after about 15 minutes of non-stop talking on my part, he held up his hand. I stopped talking. And he said, 'Son, it's no accident that we were born with two ears and only one mouth.' Needless to say, my face got red – and I stopped talking! After I apologized, I did a lot more listening.

2   **A demonstration**. When it is possible to prove the reason by demonstrating, there is little need for additional evidence. The best type of demonstration is one that gets the participants involved in proving a point under actual circumstances. There will be little doubt of the truth of a reason in the participants' minds if they play a part in making their own successful demonstration.

Example:
When teaching 'communication skills' workshops, I often demonstrate the power of silence by saying something like, 'Silence is a wonderful and powerful tool in our bag of communications tricks. In this country, we seem to have a need – almost a compulsion – to talk, rather than listen. Yet, if we are silent, we learn so much more about the other person's point of view. We can use silence by simply not talking – until the other person talks.'

   At this point, I stop talking – and wait. The pause lengthens; and finally somebody in the group will say something – demonstrating for themselves the power of silence.

3   **An exhibit**. Appealing to the sense of sight can create better understanding and faster acceptance. The old adage, 'Seeing is believing', still has a lot of merit. Showing photographs, charts, graphs or articles can help establish the reasons being offered for the learning point.

Example:
When teaching workshops on 'Time Management', I use an article by Charles E. Hummel entitled, 'The Tyranny of the Urgent'. This short, well-written article illustrates clearly the difference between those things that are 'urgent', versus those things that are truly important – and which usually gets our attention. I obtained permission from the publisher to reprint this article, and I use it as a handout to help illustrate how important it is to spend time on those things that are really important in order that we don't become 'slaves to the "tyranny of the urgent" '.

4   **The testimony of an expert**. An expert is someone who is recognized as an authority and has gained this status through demonstrated knowledge and experience. Often an article in a trade journal or a book will assist in establishing the expert classification.

Example:
When I teach Human Resource Development (HRD) classes, I often quote 'experts'. For example, when teaching Decision Making workshops, I quote Peter Drucker when discussing alternatives ('A decision to which there is only one alternative is always a bad decision'), evaluating risk ('The truly effective executive looks at all the reasons for NOT doing something before making a final decision') or compromises ('You have to know what a good compromise is – a half of a loaf of bread is still bread. A half of a baby is a dead baby.').

5   **Statistics**. Where specific data is available to prove the truth of a reason, statistics may be the answer.

Example:
When training a group of trainers, I can tell the group that copyright infringement is a serious problem in this country. But if I can also quote the statistic that '38 per cent of the videotapes that are on training shelves today are illegal copies', then the statement is more believable.

Again, using our earlier example –i.e., leaders who needed training in performance appraisal – the following is an example of step eight.

PROGRAMME DEVELOPMENT WORKSHEETS
(Page 5 of 5 pages)

Use a separate page for each objective that will be taught.
5   Objective 3: 'Given past performance records of an actual employee who works for the leader, each leader in the training session will be able to discuss the employee's strengths.'

---

6   DETERMINING REQUIRED PARTICIPANT LEARNING POINTS
List what the participants should know in order to achieve each objective. A) 'Leaders need to discuss employee's strengths in a performance appraisal interview. This is accomplished by; B) describing their specific behaviours, and illustrating with examples; C) explaining why it was important for the people involved; D) spelling out future expecta-

tions; E) expressing appreciation; and F) developing action plans to utilize the employee's strengths if appropriate.'

7 IDENTIFY REASONS FOR EACH ACKNOWLEDGED ITEM AND SKILL List the learning points and give reasons why EACH represents appropriate participant behaviour.		8 IDENTIFY EVIDENCE List appropriate analogies, demonstrations, exhibits, expert testimony or statistics for each reason.
1 Leaders need to discuss employee's positive performance in a performance appraisal session because:	– Employees need to know what their leader perceives as important. – Employees tend to continue what they are reinforced for doing. – Increases the employee's morale because most people enjoy being honestly recognized for what they do. – Increases production.	– Louis Allen's research showing that a leader's perception of the employee's job and the employee's perception of the same job are usually only 80% in agreement. – Albert Bandura's study: an average of 250% increase in desired behaviour when the subjects are given positive reinforcement. – Herzberg's study showing recognition is the third motivator as well as the second demotivator. – Ed Feeny's Emery Air Freight article.

2   Etc.
© ITC, Inc.

Notice how easy it will be to put your training programme into final form utilizing this process. Using this process for planning, the final programme will not only be of great value to the participants, but will also be fun to teach.

Step 9 – Selecting training strategies, methods and media

You conducted a well-planned needs assessment and then did a thorough job of determining your training content. Now what? Now it is time to give careful consideration to HOW the content will be taught. Most of the success or failure of a training session depends on how well the programme is designed. Good design won't guarantee success; problems will occur! But good design will immeasurably increase the odds that whatever is done will be successful. In the last step, we put it all together by carefully considering the constraints under which we work, training strategies and methods required, and the media necessary to teach the programme's content.

Designing parameters

The teaching processes we decide to use are dependent on a number of factors. For example, who has the information – the group, or the trainer? How much do the participants already know about what will be taught? How much time is available for the training session? What do we want the participants to learn? What is the skill level of the trainer? Will the climate of the organization be conducive to the teaching process selected? How many participants are in the groups that will be trained? How well do the participants know each other? What kinds of training experiences have the participants had in the past? How much money is in the budget for the programme? Who is attending?

Questions like these, all extremely important to consider in designing quality instruction, can become overwhelming. So let's organize our questions by the following classifications:

1 **Participants**
   – What do we want the participants to learn?
   – What do the participants already know about what will be taught?
   – How many participants will be in each group?
   – What is the total number of people who will be trained?
   – How well do the participants know each other?
   – What kinds of training experiences have the participants had in the past; and how do they feel about them?
   – Who is attending?
2 **Trainer**
   – How much does the trainer know about the content of the training programme?
   – What is the skill level of the trainer?

- What is the 'style' of the trainer?
- How much time does the trainer have to devote to development?

3 **Organization**
- How much money is in the budget for programme development?
- How much time is available for the training programme?
- How conducive is the 'climate' of the organization to the teaching process selected?

Of course, some of these questions will have been answered by our research on the content of the programme. But all of them must be examined in order to determine the appropriate teaching process for our group. So let's look at each of these important questions in more detail.

Participants

What do we want the participants to learn?

Very likely, in covering the first eight steps in our planning model, this question has been thoroughly answered. And the answer can tell you a lot about how to design your training programme. Suppose that your needs assessment indicated that the leaders in your organization were not managing their time effectively. You discovered during your verification interviews that these leaders were already familiar with such things as 'time logs', 'daily to-do lists' and personal planning. But you also found that even though they knew how to use these time management tools, the great majority were not doing so. Therefore, your training objective is not to teach them how to use these tools, but to determine why they don't – and to design a training programme that will lead to the actual use of good time management tools.

As you conducted your verification interviews, it also became obvious that there was a strong tendency for the leaders to blame others for their time management problems and not take responsibility for what they could control. For example, they said things like, 'What's the use of planning my time when other people constantly interrupt me?' and 'How can I plan my time when this outfit operates by crisis?'

As a result of this information, you decide to structure a learning experience that will help the participants see the need to take greater control of their lives, and accept responsibility for things that waste their time. Your final training programme should not spend time teaching participants how to do something they already know how to do. In the above instance, the programme should concern itself with helping them change their attitudes about what needs to be done – and this will require that you design a strongly experiential workshop for your participants.

To design a workshop that has a good chance of accomplishing this objective, you might choose to divide the participants into subgroups, and then have each subgroup brainstorm a list of 'all the things that waste my time'. Then show the participants a negative videotape model of someone mismanaging his or her time, and have them develop a list of all of the person's time problems.

Next ask the participants to determine which of these problems the person has some control over. Your subgroups will likely identify 85 per cent or more of the items as being within the control of the individual in the video model. Then point out the contradiction between their original lists – in which more than 85 per cent of the items are normally expressed in terms of how 'others' keep them from being effective time managers – and the lists they generated on the reasons for the video personality's time management problems.

If, on the other hand, you found that your leaders have never heard of time logs or daily to-do lists, then you will need to design a more practical, hands-on programme that would teach them *how* to use these management tools. For example, you can: 1) discuss time logs and daily to-do lists; 2) show them an example (using overhead transparencies); 3) ask for examples from the participants who have already used the ideas in managing their time; and then, 4) ask each person to commit to using a time log for three days, and a daily to-do list for one month.

As you can see, the topic, 'Time Management' is much the same for both of the above examples. But the training designs selected are entirely different based on what the participants need to learn.

What do the participants already know about what will be taught?

Of course, we have answered this question in using the planning process. But even where training is needed, the participants will likely already know *something* about the topic.

Suppose, for example, that your needs assessment clearly pointed out the need to do performance appraisal training for your organization's leaders. You can be certain that they already know something about this subject. Of course, they probably could not list the nine key steps in conducting an effective performance appraisal. And some of what they 'know' may be incorrect. But they still have some idea of what the term 'performance appraisal' means, and a general feeling concerning what they like and don't like about appraisal interviews.

What your participants already know may have a big impact on how you design the learning experiences for the group. Taking the extreme example, if your group has never heard of performance appraisals, then you probably would choose not to do group workshops where the assignment was to 'develop your own model of what an effective performance appraisal interview will look like'. So as a general rule, the more the participants already know about what is being taught, the more you can design the programme to utilize their existing knowledge. The less they know, the greater the information that will have to be presented to them.

How many participants will be in each group?

Have you tried doing a workshop with two people? Conducting such a workshop would be difficult because in groups this small, the participants' combined background is limited. In other words, the more people (within reason) that you have in your session, the greater will be the information available from the participants.

On the other hand, groups that have too many participants can also greatly affect the quality of your training sessions. Consider the effect that a group of 40 participants would have on your plans to have each person role play in front of the room and, at the same time, be recorded on video for later playback and critique by the other participants.

The number of participants in any single workshop will also determine the room size. Obviously, the more people involved, the larger the room needed.

What is the total number of people who will be trained?

In general, the more people trained, the lower the per-head cost. The number of future participants can impact such fixed cost decisions as: how much time we can afford to spend on developing the programme? How much money can we spend on audio/visual material? And how much do we want to spend on outside consultants or outside programmes? The number of people also affects our variable costs, such as the number of handout sets that will be needed, the number of sessions that need to be conducted and so forth.

How well do the participants know each other?

If your participants are strangers, then you will need to design as a part of your programme an introduction session that will help the participants get to know each other. You may choose to spend some time having each participant meet a partner whom they then introduce to the group as a whole. Or you may decide to use some form of 'ice-breaker' to reduce the tension that a group of unacquainted people normally feel.

What kind of training experiences have the participants had in the past and how do they feel about them?

Again and again, the primary concern of groups that I have facilitated has been, 'Is this going to be just another "theory" class? Or are we going to talk about the "real world"?' What I am hearing from them is a strong statement about their prior training experiences. Often you can pick up concerns like this when you conduct a needs assessment. Therefore, try to make sure that you design into the programme 'hands on', 'real world' and practical learning experiences.

Or have you ever had a learning experience such as this: 'OK, gang, each one select a partner and find a comfortable place to sit on the floor. Now, facing your partner, we are going to experience the power of "non-verbal communication". What I would like you to do is to remain absolutely silent, and to communicate by touching each other's faces while looking intently into one another's eyes.' Can you picture the above exercise being done by a group of blue-collar forepersons? Probably not! Yet when I took part in this very exercise with a group of open and trusting participants, it was an extremely moving and enriching experience for most of us.

Who is attending the training?

Sometimes the answer to this question can make a very practical difference in how you structure your training programme. For example, there seems to be a high correlation between the level of management being trained and the willingness of the training department to spend money: the higher the level, the more money is spent. Or, a particular organizational group may have special needs in the way the content is taught. Thus you may need to facilitate the same programme (i.e., same content) for different groups in very different ways. A group of engineers, for example, will likely need to be taught the same programme differently than a group of sales managers.

Trainer

How much does the trainer know about the content of the training programme?

This question may affect your design decisions in several ways. For example, suppose that your needs assessment identified 'team building' as an area of need. If you've had little experience teaching this topic, you may decide to bring in a local expert to help you with the design. Or you might decide to purchase an appropriate pre-designed off-the-shelf training package.

If you know that the future participants already have a basic knowledge of the training topic, and you are not an expert on the subject, you may decide to design the programme to be highly participative in order to tap into the group's experiences.

Of course there is a danger if you already know a lot about the training topic: your tendency may be to try to tell the participants 'everything they ever wanted to know' about the topic. This results in a poor design, with too much emphasis on giving information to the group (lecture), and not enough on involving them in the programme by encouraging participation.

What is the skill level of the trainer?

A trainer with years of experience in teaching a particular topic may be very comfortable with little structure. Give this individual a flip chart and a magic marker, a room full of people, and you might see an outstanding, participative programme with on-target group interventions and solid learning. On the other hand, a new trainer with little facilitation experience may need a great deal of structure designed into the programme. The new trainer may work best with a number of quality overhead transparencies, a detailed leader's guide and prepared group experiences that will help him or her facilitate the programme.

What is the 'style' of the trainer?

Some trainers like to lecture. Others like to have everybody sit on the floor. Some like the informality of first names; and others want to be called 'Doctor'. Some trainers like a tight schedule and others prefer a loose one.

You need to determine your own style – and then match the design of the programme to your needs. Of course, the goal is always to achieve a balance between what you need and what your participants need. You may be more comfortable lecturing; but you also realize that too much lecturing is not appropriate for your participants.

How much time does the trainer have to devote to development?

The amount of time you have to spend on development has an effect on the training design. If you had a year to spend on developing a one-day programme, you could afford to devote a great deal of effort to researching exceptional learning strategies.

For example, having budgeted two years of development time for producing this train-the-trainer programme, I had the required time to develop and validate a pre- and post-test for the facilitation section. Just writing a test was not what took the time. What required much of the time was piloting the test at three different locations. Each of the groups was divided in two, and half were initially given the pre-test, while the other half were given the post-test. Then, at the conclusion of the programme, the half that initially took the pre-test were given the post-test, and vice versa.

I then had to evaluate each of the questions. Which questions did the more knowledgeable participants get wrong? Which alternative answers (called 'distractors') did not account for a reasonable percentage of wrong answers?

These questions – and more – had to be answered before I could claim that the instrument predicts learning. And since pre- and post-tests are outstanding learning tools – participants learn more if they are looking for the needed answers during the work day – it was worth the time it took to develop them. But I had the time only because I budgeted it from the beginning!

Organization

How much money is in the budget for programme development?

Although we might agree that money won't buy happiness, it can buy well-designed training programmes! It can help provide a consultant's time to help in the development of a programme, or the creation of your own in-house videotape, or superior training facilities complete with individual computer terminals for each participant or typeset participant's manuals and quality overhead transparencies. Trainers on a tight budget might need to use more of the excellent reproducible material from University Associates, or talk to friends to find out how they might teach a specific concept (a good idea in any case) or read books on training strategies such as those listed at the end of this book.

How much time is available for the training programme?

This is a big question! Often, serious constraints are placed on the training design by the organization's need to keep people on the job. If, for example, you are given a mandate to design and develop a performance appraisal training programme, and then told that whatever you do, you must do it in half-day sessions for each group, then it is almost guaranteed that you are going to have problems – and not problems that lead to 'opportunities'! The only opportunity that you will have is to develop and design a programme that has a high probability of failing.

In general, the more time you have per group, the more time you will have for planned participation and skill development – which takes *much* time. Programmes that are not designed to be participative, and do not have plenty of opportunity for skill development, are probably not going to be judged successful.

How conducive is the 'climate' of the organization to the teaching process selected?

An unstructured learning experience that requires the participants to accept a lot of responsibility for their own direction may not be effective in an autocratic organization. And high structure may not be appropriate for a group of people who are used to setting their own agendas in the work place.

As a personal example of this, in graduate school I was with the same group of 'HRD-type' people for three years, and developed a close relationship with this group. In addition, most of the classes that we took together were in the university's School of Education adult department. This department had a strong adult learning orientation, and wisely encouraged our growth through freedom of expression, challenging discussions and other participative techniques. Unfortunately, we were assigned a professor who seemed to have forgotten everything he ever knew about good training. We got dry, boring lectures; and he got a 'revolt'!

Training strategies

We can better select appropriate training strategies if we look at the three main sections of a training programme – the opening, the body and the closing. This is because the strategy selected depends on our participants' needs, and their needs are different depending on where they are in a training session.

Opening

Nervous laughter. Animated movement. And then stillness as you begin your training session. These are some of the behaviours you can expect to encounter at the beginning of your training session. Why? Anxiety! The participants may not know each other – or you. They may not know what is expected of them. Some have had bad training experiences in the past. So they are anxious. And maybe you are, too!

Do you remember the principle, 'A good training design reduces the tension felt by the participants?' It tells you that design strategies will be needed in your programme to deal with the participants' entry feelings.

Opening strategies are needed for the following reasons.

Reduce participant tension

One idea is to write out a participant's 'Bill of Rights' on flip chart paper, and then post this list on the wall before the session. Consider a list something like this:

PARTICIPANT'S BILL OF RIGHTS
You have the right to:
– ask questions
– have your questions answered
– offer suggestions and ideas
– have opinions and ideas that are different than mine
– be listened to
– not be embarrassed by the facilitator or other participants
– choose not to participate.

Another strategy for reducing the participants' tension is providing the participants with their 'place' when they first enter the training room. For example, you could have name tags pre-printed with each participant's name already placed on one of the tables. This has the added advantage of allowing you to position the participants beside people they already know (or don't know, depending on your objective), separate a participant who may work for another participant or put intact work groups together. If possible, you could match up the participants' names with their faces and be able to greet them by name when they enter the room.

You can also reduce the participant's initial tension by sending out in advance of the programme the course objectives, a detailed outline and location directions. For a participant to discover at the last minute that he or she doesn't know where the programme is being presented can raise the tension of even the calmest participant.

Other strategies – such as creating connections between the participants, modelling personal disclosures, and group work used to develop expectations and reservations – can also reduce the participant's tension. Let us look briefly at these.

Create connections between the participants.

A simple round-robin introduction session can aid in reducing participant tension. For example, you can write out in advance several questions, like:

● What is your name?
● What do you do in your job?
● What interests or hobbies do you have outside of your job?

- What do you feel are your job-related strengths?
- Why are you here today?

Then have the participants pair up and interview one another for three minutes per person, followed by each participant introducing his or her partner to the rest of the group.

There are a number of variations of this basic strategy. You could give each participant a 'Bingo' card, and then have them move around interviewing each other, until they find people that fill all of the descriptions on the card. A sample card is shown in Figure 2.

Model personal disclosures

If it is important for the participants to be 'real' with each other during the programme, then one good way of making that happen is for you to model the behaviours you want to see. When you first introduce yourself to the group you can talk about your own anxieties about being the trainer, personal things from your own background that may impact the group and some of your bad experiences as a participant in past training programmes. Here is an example of some of the things that I have said to past groups:

'BINGO NAMEGO'

Locate individuals in the room who match the following statements. Write the individuals' names in the appropriate boxes. The person who has the most names on his or her card after 7 minutes is the winner. (Note that an individual's name can appear more than once on your 'Bingo Namego' card. Your name, however, should not appear on your card.)

Took violin lessons	Likes pets	Hates pets	Was born in New York	Likes Greek food	Enjoys the symphony
———	———	———	———	———	———
Married the longest	Has a sports car	Can water ski	Has ridden a snowmobile	Has been to Niagara Falls	Collects coins
———	———	———	———	———	———
Has the most children	Has metric tools	Owns a personal computer	Loves to cook	Owned a 57 Chevy	Likes being single
———	———	———	———	———	———

Figure 2 Sample 'Bingo' card

Good morning. My name is Dick Leatherman. I do prefer first names, so 'Dick' will be fine. I had an opportunity to meet each of you as you arrived this morning, and I'm excited about being with you today. I'm excited because today's topic is one of my favourites, and also one I feel very qualified to teach. I'm also a little nervous, mostly because I tend to be shy, and I don't know many of you yet. But don't worry – I'm not going to have an anxiety attack and run screaming out of this room! As we work together today, we'll get to know each other better, and I'll feel more comfortable.

You need to know a couple of things about me – personal things – because they will have an impact on you today. First, I can't spell. I mean, I really can't! And this is not a 'self-fulfilling prophecy'. You know what that is: I believe I can't spell, and therefore I never bothered to learn how. I was born dyslexic, long before this particular disorder became commonly known.

But my problem with spelling is a real opportunity for you – for two reasons. First, because of my spelling difficulties, I *hate* to take notes. As a result, you are going to receive a set of prepared handouts, which means you don't have to take notes unless you want to. Trust me! You'll get handouts on everything that I cover today.

Second, I am not going to write on that easel any more than I have to, because I don't want to make a fool out of myself. Instead, I will be using overhead transparencies throughout the day. And I think you'll like them. They are professionally prepared and easy to read. And the nice thing about transparencies is that I won't take up your time writing everything down.

One last point before we move into today's topic. In the list of objectives I sent you last week, some of you may have noticed that we will be doing some role play later this afternoon. In programmes that I've attended in the past as a participant, as soon as somebody mentioned 'role play', my anxieties immediately increased. So let me give you some information now about how our role play session will be conducted. First, you will be given ample time to prepare for the practice session. Second, subgroups will be practising simultaneously at their own tables. Nobody is going to be asked to stand up in front of the room and role play. When you practise, for example, you four people at table one will be practising at the same time as tables two and three, etc.

As you can see, self-disclosure can set the stage for openness on the part of the participants. It also helps to accomplish the next strategy: reducing your role as the 'teacher'.

Reduce your role as the 'teacher'

Unfortunately, not all participants have fond memories of their early school years. So anything you can do to reduce a participant's projection of past negative experiences on to you as a 'teacher', the better! Using self-disclosure helps because teachers don't usually talk like I talked in the above example. Communicating to the participants that this is THEIR programme (as evidenced by the up-front needs assessment that you conducted), not yours, will also help in minimizing the 'teacher' role.

Determine the participants' expectations and/or reservations

In advance of your programme, you can design an introduction transparency (or flip chart) like that in Figure 3.

A transparency (or flip chart) such as this will help the participants reduce their tension by working together – while also giving you important information to use in conducting the programme and setting the stage for a participative workshop.

Present your expectations

In planning this portion of the workshop, you can write out your expectations on a flip chart. At the beginning of the programme, review each expectation with the participants. This list of expectations can then be posted on a wall so that it will be clearly visible to the participants during the programme.

You might include expectations like:

I expect you to ...
– be on time
– plan to stay until the programme is over
– make arrangements with your office so that we are not interrupted
– refrain from reading the handouts ahead of time

---

1   FORM GROUPS OF 4 OR 5 PER TABLE.

2   ELECT A LEADER AT EACH TABLE.

3   YOU HAVE 6 MINUTES TO ANSWER THE FOLLOWING TWO QUESTIONS (3 MIN. PER QUESTION):

  – WHAT DO YOU HOPE TO GAIN FROM ATTENDING THIS PROGRAMME (YOUR EXPECTATIONS)?
  – WHAT ARE YOUR HONEST RESERVATIONS OR CONCERNS ABOUT BEING IN THIS PROGRAMME?

4   LEADERS: PLEASE WRITE YOUR GROUP'S RESPONSES DIRECTLY ON THE FLIP CHART PAPER.

5   AT THE CONCLUSION OF THE 6-MINUTE TIME PERIOD, THE LEADER AT EACH TABLE WILL REPORT HIS OR HER TABLES COMMENTS.

6   THE FIRST TIME AROUND. THE LEADERS WILL REPORT THE GROUP'S EXPECTATIONS. THEN RESERVATIONS OR CONCERNS WILL BE REPORTED.

Figure 3   Introduction transparency

- contribute to today's discussion
- be respectful of other participant's ideas
- listen to one another
- stay awake.

Give administrative details

When are breaks scheduled? Where are the toilets? What time do we eat? When is the programme over? These are examples of 'administrative' questions that the facilitator needs to answer when opening the programme. The answers to these questions can be written out in advance on a flip chart or overhead transparency. This will keep you from inadvertently forgetting to mention a key item to the participants.

Body

To design the body of our training programme, we will use the four 'As': ask, advise, assimilate and apply. A specific block of programme content can be taught by first *asking* the participants for information (their experiences with the topic, concerns about the topic, etc.), and then *advising* – presenting information to the participants (about the objectives, content, etc.). We next give the participants an opportunity to *assimilate* the information that was presented (subgroup work, discussions, etc.). And last, the participants are given time in the programme to *apply* the information to their jobs (through role play, practice, etc.).

We have suggested above that the four 'As' be used in a specific block of the programme, because it is normally not advisable to present a full day's programme as one complete unit. A far better design is to break the programme up into discrete units, and then facilitate each unit using the four 'As'. Thus, you will need to use the four-step process numerous times during the programme. Let's discuss each of the four steps in more detail.

Asking

This step sounds like a needs assessment; and in one way it is. It is an assessment of the participants' knowledge about the specific content that is about to be taught. You can look at the needs assessment that you conducted prior to the programme as a 'macro' study, and this classroom assessment as a 'micro' study. This step is not something you do only once at the beginning of the programme (e.g., an 'expectation/reservation' exercise), but should be used throughout the session each time you present a new block of programme content.

We use the 'asking' step for the following reasons:

1   It acknowledges the strengths of the participants by expressing interest in their existing knowledge through asking and listening.
2   It may reduce training time by revealing what the participants already know.
3   It can reveal previous experience that might interfere with new learning.
4   It may disclose prior experience to which new learning can be related.

The idea is NOT just a quick, 'What have you experienced before?' to set up your presentation. The facilitator must have a real desire to probe for any possible past experience that can be related to the new information that will be presented.

If, for example, you were facilitating a class on 'How to Make Transparencies', you might first ask, 'What's been your experience with overhead transparencies?' Either you obtain information or you don't. If you do, then you can use that past experience to help explain your new information.

If you don't get a response to your question, you will probably change that particular line of questioning. You might ask, 'What – if any – kinds of programmes have you attended where transparencies were used?' And, 'What were some of the things you liked about transparencies?' Whatever information you obtain, you listen actively, nodding your head saying, 'I see' etc., at appropriate points without interrupting. Follow up with questions like, 'Can you be more specific?', 'Could you give me an example?' or 'How was that done?'

Thus, as a part of your planning you need not only to allow time for the above discussion, but also to write out questions on the topic in advance of the programme. You might even place the participants in subgroups, and give them an assignment using an overhead transparency, such as in Figure 4.

---

1   IN SUBGROUPS OF 4 TO 5 PARTICIPANTS. ELECT NEW LEADERS AND ANSWER THE FOLLOWING QUESTIONS ON YOUR FLIP CHART PAPER (5 MINUTES):

  – WHAT EXPERIENCES HAVE THE INDIVIDUALS IN YOUR GROUP HAD IN MAKING TRANSPARENCIES?
  – WHAT KINDS OF PROGRAMMES HAVE YOU ATTENDED WHERE TRANSPARENCIES WERE USED? (EXCLUDE THIS PROGRAMME)
  – WHAT WERE THE THINGS YOU LIKED ABOUT USING TRANSPARENCIES?
  – WHAT WERE THE THINGS YOU DID NOT LIKE ABOUT USING TRANSPARENCIES?

2   THE LEADERS WILL THEN REPORT THEIR GROUP'S FINDINGS.

Figure 4   Assignment transparency

Advising

'Advising' is a step many trainers feel they are well prepared to facilitate. But this is frequently not the case. Because it seems so easy for us to 'tell' our participants EVERYTHING they need to know about a training topic, we tend to talk too much. As we have already indicated, part of this problem is solved by careful needs assessment, followed by deleting anything the participants in fact already know.

We also can avoid our potential 'talking' problems by carefully asking key questions about the participants' experience just prior to presenting training information. And we should also note that even the 'Asking' step can contribute to a talking problem. It's as if we say, 'OK, I've listened to YOU. Now it's MY turn to talk.'

Therefore, protect yourself – and your participants – by designing training strategies that will force you to be participative, even in the 'Advising' section of the training programme. Obtain and use alternate forms of presentation, such as a videotape to augment your presentation, and transparencies or flip charts to guide you and your participants in a subgroup discussion. In the next section, we will discuss the variety of media and methods you can consider utilizing as you plan your training programme.

Assimilating

After advising, we should provide opportunities for the participants to *assimilate* the information we have presented. Participants come to a training programme with particular sets of experiences. Some of their experiences will help them learn new material; and others will block their learning. Thus they need opportunities to compare the information you have presented with what they have previously experienced, and to integrate the new knowledge with their past experience.

In this stage, subgroup work and open, general discussions are two methods that can be used to help the participants assimilate new information. Suppose, for example, that you were facilitating a programme on how to conduct performance appraisal interviews. It is the morning of the first day, and you are dealing with the need for participative interviews. You ask the participants about their experiences with participative interviews, and you discover that although some of them feel they have been participative in conducting interviews, others are strongly opposed to conducting participative interviews. The latter group feels that employees should be called in, seated and tactfully told their strengths and weaknesses. (Note that this response by some of the participants is not a surprise to you, because you have already discovered this viewpoint during your initial needs assessment and confirmed it when you then conducted verification interviews.) At this point you need to present reasons why it is more effective to conduct performance appraisal interviews WITH employees – and then give the participants an opportunity to assimilate the information.

Fortunately, you did your homework. You knew that there was a high probability that some of the participants would have difficulty accepting this new way of conducting appraisal interviews. So you have already planned a process and allowed time to help them deal with it. You have created the following transparency in Figure 5.

Using this process, you will give the participants time to assimilate the new information, and use the experience of the group to assist those who hold more authoritarian views. It often takes time to accept and integrate new information. So give your participants a chance to deal with their feelings in incorporating new knowledge into their fund of experience.

Applying

You can read a book on windsurfing, watch someone windsurf and even write an article on 'The Joys of Riding the Wind'. But you cannot understand what wind-surfing is really all about until you actually do it yourself. Similarly, your participants can't learn how to apply new knowledge to their jobs by just reading. They can't truly learn simply by watching you or someone else. They must actually apply the knowledge themselves and receive accurate feedback on their application. Thus the application step is critical, and should be designed into the programme.

In the section on 'Methods', you will learn several ways to help the participants apply the information you have presented in training.

---

1   FORM SUBGROUPS OF 4 OR 5 AND ELECT A LEADER.

2   YOUR GROUP HAS 10 MINUTES TIME TO:

A   LIST ON ONE SHEET OF FLIP CHART PAPER ALL THE REASONS YOU CAN THINK OF FOR CONDUCTING A **PARTICIPATIVE** PERFORMANCE APPRAISAL INTERVIEW (5 MINUTES).

B   ON A SECOND SHEET OF FLIP CHART PAPER, LIST AS MANY REASONS AS YOU CAN FOR CONDUCTING A PERFORMANCE APPRAISAL INTERVIEW IN WHICH THE EMPLOYEE'S PARTICIPATION IS MINIMAL (5 MINUTES).

C   WHICH OF THE ABOVE TWO METHODS OF CONDUCTING APPRAISAL INTERVIEWS DOES YOUR GROUP PREFER TO USE?

3   BE PREPARED TO REPORT ON YOUR GROUP'S WORK AND TO DEFEND ITS POSITION.

Figure 5   Assimilation transparency

Closing

Three areas can be addressed at the close of a training programme: 1) the past, (evaluating the programme); 2) the present (Where are we now?); and, 3) the future (Where are we going?). You may choose to address all three areas or one or two of them, depending on the time that is available.

The past

Here, several different programme factors can be evaluated. First, the participants may evaluate themselves and how well they reached their own objectives. This can be accomplished by designing a group exercise in which the participants are asked to review their initial expectations and/or reservations. Of course, this exercise requires that the participants have expressed their expectations and reservations when the programme started. For example, you can make a transparency or flip chart as in Figure 6.

You may also ask the participants to evaluate how well you have facilitated the programme. For example, you could have each participant identify one thing he or she liked about the way you conducted the session, and one thing he/she wished you had done differently. Then, in triads (or larger groups, if you prefer), ask the participants to discuss their comments and select the thing they liked best about the programme, as well as the most important thing they wish you had done differently. Next, ask each subgroup to give you feedback, starting with the things they wished you had done differently. When each of the groups has reported their first item, have them take turns reporting the thing they each liked best about the way you facilitated the programme.

The participants can also be asked to evaluate the programme itself. Here we are not referring to the formal written evaluations often completed at the close of a programme, but to an open discussion which helps the participants obtain closure. (The word 'closure' means to feel finished,

---

1   ELECT NEW LEADERS FOR EACH TABLE.

2   YOU HAVE 5 MINUTES TO ANSWER THE FOLLOWING TWO QUESTIONS (2½ MIN. PER QUESTION):

   – HOW WELL DID WE MEET YOUR EXPECTATIONS? (BE VERY SPECIFIC IN YOUR COMMENTS.)
   – HOW DO YOU FEEL NOW ABOUT THE RESERVATIONS THAT YOU HAD WHEN THE PROGRAMME STARTED? (AGAIN, BE SPECIFIC.)

3   LEADERS WILL REPORT THEIR GROUP'S COMMENTS.

Figure 6   Evaluation exercise

or to have completed a main task.) To accomplish this, you may ask the participants to consider which topics were especially valuable, and which were not; which topics deserved more time, and which less; and which should have been covered that weren't. You can design in advance of the programme a transparency or flip chart stating these questions, to help facilitate this discussion.

The present

It has been a long day. But there is a feeling of accomplishment, of doing something important – together. If you take the time to recognize and process these feelings, it can help the participants achieve closure. You may use a simple exercise like asking the participants to individually write down, and then comment on, the most important thing gained from the programme. Or you can ask each participant to write a statement that describes what he or she is feeling at this moment, and then ask each one to express what he/she wrote. Here you also should write out what you are feeling and be the first to volunteer to report what you wrote. (The participants should also be told that they are free not to comment if they so choose.)

Another effective closing technique is to ask the participants to provide positive feedback to one another. Pair up the participants, and have each person write a positive statement about his or her partner. Then each participant in turn reads – and comments on – what he or she wrote about his or her partner.

There are a number of variations of this exercise. For example, you may ask the participants to spend one minute thinking about what they learned from, or appreciated about, their partner during the programme. Then have the participants express to the group their thoughts about their partners.

Another helpful strategy is to give the participants an opportunity to say goodbye to each other. This is especially important if they have been together for several days. Ask them to quietly look around the room and note those people that they are especially going to miss, and to consider why they will be missed. Then suggest that when the group is ready, they stand and go to the people they identified, one at a time, and say goodbye. When they have finished, they may leave. (Ask to be included in this goodbye exercise. It is a powerful experience!)

The future

One of the ways that you can keep your programme from becoming just another 'happiness programme' (happiness programmes make everybody happy – but without change) is to help the participants build bridges from the classroom to the job. One of the best ways to do this is to have them determine what it is they want to do differently on the job (goal-setting), and then develop step-by-step plans to achieve their goals. You will probably need to create and design this strategy before you do your programme. For example, you might first design a handout such as that shown in Figure 7.

After designing the handout, make a transparency of it and write in an example using a transparency marking pen. In addition, prepare another transparency as in Figure 8.

At the close of the workshop, pass out the assignment, show the transparency that you prepared as an example of the handout, and then show the transparency you designed to give the participants their instructions.

When the participants have completed their work, call on each one, asking them to share just one of their ideas and related mini-action plan.

Another objective you may have is to encourage the participants to stay in touch with one another. Participants often reinforce their learning by interacting with each other back on the job. An example of this strategy is to continue the above exercise as follows: as each participant offers one idea and action plan, you ask if another participant will volunteer to have a follow-up meeting with the first participant to discuss how well they have accomplished their action plan. Or you could simply ask the participants to exchange phone numbers for the purpose of keeping in touch.

Now that we have looked at strategies for the opening, body and close of a training programme, let's turn to training methods and media that can be used to help us implement these strategies.

Training methods

Let us now examine some of the training methods which are frequently suggested in train-the-trainer books – focusing on those which are most popularly utilized.

In general, we can look at training methods as being on a continuum of *participant involvement*, which moves from 'presentation of information' at one end to 'leaderless groups' at the other. Let's first look at the two ends of this continuum, and then at some of the training methods that fall between these two points.

Presentations

There are a number of things you can do in your designing stage to help you be a better presenter for your participants. First, there is nothing wrong with a group training presentation style. There are times when it is very appropriate for the trainer simply to present information to the group.

IDEA 1	IDEA 2	IDEA 3
ACTION PLAN	ACTION PLAN	ACTION PLAN
1	1	1
2	2	2
3	3	3
4	4	4
5	5	5

Figure 7 Action plan for personal improvement

```
1   PLEASE TAKE 8 MINUTES TO COMPLETE THE 'ACTION PLAN' WORKSHEET
    AS FOLLOWS:

    – SELECT AT LEAST THREE THINGS THAT YOU HAVE LEARNED IN THIS
      PROGRAMME THAT WILL HELP YOU BACK ON THE JOB.
    – WRITE A 'MINI' ACTION PLAN TO PUT INTO PRACTICE EACH OF THE
      IDEAS.

2   YOU WILL THEN BE ASKED TO PUBLICLY COMMIT TO ONE OF YOUR
    THREE IDEAS.
```

Figure 8   Action plan transparency

But note that this type of training has – justifiably – increasingly received a 'bad press' because of its main drawback: it can become boring to the participant.

An information-presentation style of training does not have to be boring. But too much of it can put your participants to sleep! It takes a good 'edutainer' (my term for education that is entertaining) to keep participants' attention for more than 15 minutes of lecture. So when using this method of teaching, turn your lectures into 'lecturettes'. In other words, break a lecture up into shorter segments – and have the participants do something with what they have just learned before moving on to the next segment.

In addition, use examples, analogies and even parables to make the presentation portion of your programme as interesting as possible. Using a parable, for instance, is an excellent way of giving advice that participants will accept, and remember. Consider the master storyteller who wished to say, 'Celebrate that which is lost and then found'. His training method was a parable: 'If a man owns a hundred sheep, and one of them wanders away, will he not leave the ninety-nine on the hills and go to look for the one that wandered off? And if he finds it, … he is happier about that one sheep than about the ninety-nine that did not wander off.'

Or look at another example. Suppose I am teaching 'Introduction to Management' at the local university, and the topic for today's class is 'Participative vs. Autocratic Leadership'. The point I wish to make to the class is that many leaders talk about participative leadership, but too often what they say and what they do are entirely different. So I tell the following story:

> Once upon a time there was a manager who believed in the power of participative leadership. In fact, he would tell everyone, at every opportunity, how wonderfully participative he was, at all times, with his people. Then one day he learned that there was going to be a surprise audit of his section sometime within the week. So the first thing he did was to sit quietly in his office and

list all those things he thought the auditors would examine. Then he evaluated each item to see what potential problems might exist. Next, he determined appropriate solutions for each of the problem areas. Finally, he identified who on his staff could best handle each problem.

He then called a meeting of his supervisors and told them of the impending audit, and of the problems that the auditors might uncover and what the supervisors should do. He asked each of his key people to give it their best, and to do what needed to be done as quickly as possible. 'After all,' he said, 'I want – and need – your participation on this.'

At this point, as the trainer I would lead a discussion on what participative management really means, and the impact that emergencies have on what we do. After discussing these issues, I might even tell another story:

> Now let me change the story about our participative manager. He had learned about the surprise audit as he was leaving the organization's car park to go home. As he was driving home, he noticed a dark, ominous cloud forming in the sky above his car. Suddenly there was a mighty flash of lightning, which struck his car. And as the thunder rumbled and roared, our hero was miraculously changed into a truly participative manager. He was aware! Aware of a whole new way of looking at the world – and at the way he managed. The next morning, when he arrived at the organization, what do you think he did?

Here, I might lead another discussion about what managers really do when they operate as participative leaders. The messages I would draw out of the parable are: 1) people often don't know how others perceive them; and 2) people can change – even without being hit by lightning.

When you create parables and analogies, be sure that they relate to the content that will be taught – i.e., your learning objective. Then, practice being informal in your style of delivery, even though your material is highly planned.

Unless you have conducted a given workshop many times, you will need to have some type of notes to use as a guide in your presentation of information to the participants. One suggestion here: don't write out a 'script', even if it is the first time you are facilitating the programme. By the time you complete the planning process discussed earlier, you are going to be fairly expert on the topic you are presenting. At least you are going to know a great deal more about the subject than your participants.

But our tendency is to write out great amounts of information so that we 'won't forget'. And we end up presenting far too much information to the participants.

The best strategy is to make an outline, and then simply speak from it. If you are using overhead transparencies, your job is simple because the transparencies become your notes. Put your outline on the transparencies, write any additional notes on the transparency frames, and you will be amazed at how well you will remember the things you need to say. And having your notes on the transparency frames will allow you to maintain good eye contact with the group during this presentation portion of your programme.

Leaderless groups

This method involves having a small number of people (usually 6 to 14) sit in a circle with the leader as a member of the group. But the leader does NOT 'lead'. In fact, he or she will usually say nothing! This forces the group to struggle to define itself and what it wants to accomplish (if anything), while the leader, for the most part, stays out of it. The leader's only active role is to facilitate discussion by acting as a catalyst when all else fails.

Leaderless groups can be fascinating – and demanding! My suggestion is that this training method is generally for illustrative purposes only (representing one end of our continuum). Don't attempt to facilitate a leaderless group until you have had ample training in doing so.

General discussions

One of the most popular methods to use in a training programme is to lead a general discussion with the participants. General discussions can be used to:

- *Obtain information from the participants.* For instance, at the beginning of your programme you may want to discover what the participants already know about the topics that will be taught. After presenting the programme's objectives, you could ask the group, 'What has been your past experience with these objectives?' At this point, you will simply need to lead a general discussion, encouraging as many participants as possible to speak in the time allowed.
- *Lead the group to discover for itself a particular concept.* For example, you are facilitating a programme on 'Problem-Solving With Employees', and you have just stated, 'It is important to involve our employees in discussing the cause of a problem that concerns them.' Then you ask, 'Why is that important?' At this point you can encourage a general discussion of the reason for involving employees in causal analysis. Of course, you could simply have told them why this is important. But it is much more interesting and enlightening for trainees if they have an opportunity to participate in the discussion.
- *Handle group disagreement.* During a training programme a participant

may state an opinion which is contrary to what you (or another participant) has already expressed. You can, of course, tell the participant how wrong he or she is, and give 68 reasons why your original statement is correct! But it will be much more effective to let the group handle the divergent member by asking, 'How do the rest of you feel about that?' Then sit back and enjoy a participative discussion. Remember: what you need is more information. If an individual in the group is not 'buying into' what has been presented, then you *need* to know as much as possible about how this participant – and others – feel. And the best way to discover new information is to ask a question, close your mouth and open your ears!

Brainstorming

In its basic form, brainstorming is simply a way of generating a large amount of information from the participants through posing a question, and then recording – without judgement – all of the ideas that are suggested. Suppose, for example, that you are teaching a group 'decision-making' skills. You have just talked about the need to have creative alternatives when making decisions. At this point in the programme you might appoint a recording secretary (this leaves you free to facilitate the discussion), pose a hypothetical decision statement and ask the group to generate as many alternatives as possible. You also instruct the group not to make *any* negative comments about anyone's suggestion, no matter how silly it might sound; and, as the list grows longer, to look at ideas that have been suggested in order to generate new thoughts. You also ask the recording secretary to write down on flip chart paper *every* idea that is expressed.

Encourage the group to come up with as many ideas as possible. When they are finished, hang the list of suggestions on the wall. Then ask the group to examine the list of ideas to determine which are feasible, which are not, and which might be combined to make even better alternatives. Ask the recording secretary to write down the final alternative statements as they are suggested by the group.

Buzz groups

Buzz groups are normally temporary teams of two to three participants that are given a particular topic or question to discuss, and then report to the group as a whole. Such subgroups are used to generate easy discussion and to obtain a wide range of ideas from a group of participants. This is an excellent strategy to use with newly formed groups or with participants who seem shy with each other – or with you. If trainees have an opportunity to discuss an assignment with one or two partners 'privately', it makes it easier for them to then participate in a general discussion.

Subgroups

Subgroups, as defined here, are simply large buzz groups, and serve much the same purpose as buzz groups. Usually, subgroups are composed of four to six participants who are seated together at a table. (If you have 20 participants in a session, you will probably set up the tables and chairs so that there were five trainees at each of four tables, as shown in Figure 9.

Following are some important suggestions concerning facilitating sub-groups:

1   Since you will know in advance that the participants will be forming into subgroups, set up the room to make it easy for them to do so. If your tables are set up in either a 'V' or a 'U' configuration, place extra chairs on the inside of the 'V' or 'U' to accommodate the subgroups; or even set up separate subgroup tables with chairs. If the participants will be spending a significant amount of time in subgroups, then it may be best to seat them at separate tables of four or five participants each at the start (as shown in Figure 9).
2   If the people have to move around to get into their groups, let them first move before giving them their task instructions.
3   Ask each group to elect a leader or spokesperson. (You need somebody to be IN CHARGE of each subgroup.)

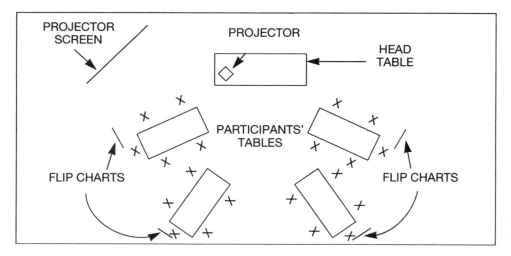

Figure 9   Subgroup seating arrangement

4   Provide flip chart paper, magic markers and masking tape for each sub-group. Ask that the leaders appoint secretaries who will record ideas directly on the paper as they are generated by their groups. (Request that the secretaries do not make notes on note paper and later try to transfer them to flip chart paper since they will not have the time to do so.)

5   Make your instructions clearly visible by putting them on an overhead transparency or flip chart, or having them pre-written on a blackboard. Write out:
   - how you want the groups organized – i.e., elect leaders, appoint recording secretaries, etc.
   - time constraints
   - groups' task assignment.

6   After reviewing the instructions, ask for questions before starting to work.

7   While the subgroups are working, be highly visible. Walk around and visit each subgroup to ensure that the work is going smoothly.

8   When the subgroup report their work to the group as a whole, suggest that each report be a concise, abbreviated overview of what that specific group accomplished. Lengthy reports can become extremely boring to other participants.

9   At the end of the report period, ask for 'minority reports' to make sure that anyone who has a burning issue that wasn't written down has the opportunity to express it.

Testing

You may wonder why 'testing' is listed as a training method. Consider this: if prior to a training session your participants take a pre-test which covers the material that will be presented, then they are going to be very attentive when each pre-test question's material is covered during the day. Thus it is often worthwhile to spend time designing a multiple-choice questionnaire to use as a pre-test.

Writing a multiple-choice questionnaire is not easy. And normally, if you are going to write a pre-test, it is beneficial also to write a post-test so that you can measure your participants' learning. (Pre- and post-test construction and analysis is covered in the 'Evaluation' section of this module.) If writing one test is hard work, writing two tests is even more so. The following hints may assist you in developing a test (or instrument) for your participants:

1   Make your test multiple-choice. A test should measure actual *knowledge* of the subject that is to be taught, not someone's 'perception' of what

they know or don't know. A perception test, or instrument, is nothing more than a series of topic statements which asks the test-taker to indicate the degree to which they know the topic. For example, a perception-type pre-test on 'Training Media' might look like this:

Indicate the degree to which you agree or disagree with the following statements.
[Indicate 'Strongly agree' (SA), 'Agree' (A), 'Disagree' (D) or 'Strongly disagree' (SD).]

I need to know more about:	*SA*	*A*	*D*	*SD*
Using the overhead projector	——	——	——	——
Making transparencies	——	——	——	——
Writing handouts	——	——	——	——
Preparing flip charts	——	——	——	——
Using the tape recorder	——	——	——	——
Etc.	——	——	——	——

As you can see, this turns into nothing more than a mini-needs assessment analysis. The problem with this form of 'testing' is that it doesn't give the test-taker an opportunity to determine his or her real knowledge-level – only one's perception of his or her knowledge.

Thus, the topic 'Using the overhead projector' will be checked 'Strongly disagree' by most participants because the test-taker's perception probably is: 'What is there to learn about a simple overhead projector?' But there is much to learn about projectors. And if you wrote several multiple-choice questions to determine what the test-taker really knows about them, the likelihood is that both of you would see a need for more information in this area.

For example, below are two multiple-choice questions on 'Using the overhead projector' that will demonstrate the point above:

Select the *most* appropriate reason for the following statements:
1 It is important not to jar an overhead projector when it is on because:
   a) It can move the image out of focus.
   b) It makes the image out of focus.
   c) The filament is soft when the light is on, and easily breaks.
   d) The projector can shift slightly on the table or stand, which moves the image off the screen.

2 The main reason for using overhead transparencies, rather than a blackboard and chalk, is because they:
   a) Make it easier to maintain eye contact with the group.

b) Increase the amount of information that can be transmitted in a given period of time.

c) Increase the participants' retention of the programme's ideas and concepts.

d) Clearly communicates to the participants that you care enough about them and the programme to go to the trouble of obtaining transparencies.

[The answers are: 1c, 2b.]

From the above example, you may agree that the information obtained by using a multiple-choice questionnaire is considerably more accurate than what is learned from a perception-type instrument.

2 Avoid 'trivia' questions. Write your multiple-choice questions on the *key* content that will be taught. If you first determine what should be taught and then write the participant's manual, you will have a good idea of exactly what content the pre- and post-test questions should cover. Thus, test construction should be one of the last things you do in designing your programme.

3 Pilot your test. Even the best communicators in writing find that their initial efforts produce questions that few people understand, questions that everybody gets right – or wrong, distractors (the three wrong answers) that don't distract anybody and questions that the most knowledgeable participants get wrong!

After you pilot your test with a sample group, conduct a 'frequency count' on each question's answers, i.e., how many people in the group selected 'a' as the answer, how many selected 'b' and so forth. The frequency count will help you decide which questions are well-designed, which need rewriting and which questions are beyond hope!

You may use the following criteria:

– Delete, or rewrite, any distractor that isn't chosen by at least 5 per cent of the test-takers.

– Delete, or rewrite, any questions that more than 90 per cent of the test-takers get wrong, or 90 per cent get right. (Such questions don't discriminate between the well-informed and ill-informed test-taker.)

4 If all the multiple-choice responses to a question or statement begin with the same words, then put those words in the question or statement. For example, look at the immediately preceding paragraph. Note that the words 'delete, or rewrite, any' appear in both criteria statements. The better wording is:

You may use the following criteria: delete, or rewrite, any

- distractor that isn't chosen by at least 5 per cent of the test-takers.
- a question that more than 90 per cent of the test-takers get wrong, or 90 per cent get right.

This will make it easier for the participants to read the question and choices, and will take less time for them to complete the test.

5   When composing the multiple-choices for a question, avoid using words like 'always' or 'never'. These words are strong signals that this answer is incorrect.

6   Be alert for 'give-aways' – i.e., the lead provides clues for the answer. For example, one can easily select the most correct answer in the following question with no knowledge of training content.

> Training is a:
> a)   difficult job.
> b)   rewarding profession.
> c)   awesome responsibility.
> d)   thankless task.

Did you select the correct answer ('c')? The only choice that 'Training is AN ...' matches in terms of good English usage is 'awesome responsibility'.

Another example of a clue built into the lead is the following:

> A professional trainer is involved in:
> a)   a difficult job.
> b)   a rewarding profession.
> c)   organizational politics.
> d)   a thankless task.

This question has two problems. The word 'professional' in the lead points to the word 'profession' in answer 'b'. In addition, answers 'a', 'c' and 'd' are negative in tone, while answer 'b' is more positive. Even a poor 'test-taker' can correctly guess this one!

7   If possible, avoid 'none of the above' as well as 'all of the above' as choices. These phrases are often used when the test-designer runs out of ideas for good distractors.

8   Twenty questions covering a one-day programme is probably more than adequate. You need enough questions to reasonably cover the content, but not so many that the participants spend too much training time in test-taking. You may estimate that each multiple-choice question will take about 45 seconds to answer, which means that a 20-question test will take about 15 minutes to complete – not counting time needed to introduce, distribute and collect the test.

Case studies

The case study training method has been used for years to help participants make the transition from knowledge to application. The cases may be real or imaginary, just as long as they fit the application required. 'Real' cases, if obtained from within the organization, should be disguised if possible. An imaginary case should have its setting match that of the organization. Most imaginary cases can be easily rewritten to fit the organizational environment. In general, the closer the cases match your organizational environment, the better the participants will relate to them.

If you decide to write your own cases, try to strike a balance between providing enough information for the participants to apply the case, and not so much detail that it takes more time to read the case than it does to use it.

Since case analysis is often done best when the participants are placed in subgroups, use the same methods discussed earlier in presenting the case to the group – i.e., use transparencies or prepared flip charts to present the instructions to the group. An additional technique useful in case analysis is to first have the participants individually read the case and attempt to write their own answers to the case's questions, and then break them down into subgroups so they can share their answers and arrive at a composite response in each group.

Modelling

Modelling is a way of demonstrating a specific behaviour or set of behaviours that has just been learned. This method of training was first made popular in the early 1900s as a way of teaching employee job skills by: 1) *telling* the employee how to do a job, 2) *showing* the employee how to do it (modelling) and 3) letting the employee *practise* what was explained and demonstrated.

Today, trainers use three strategies that involve modelling:

1   You, the trainer, can model behaviours for your participants by demonstrating what you have taught. If, for example, you have just taught your participants how to give feedback that was non-judgemental, you can model this behaviour by actually giving the class non-judgemental feedback. Suppose your group has been very passive – not asking questions or offering opinions, even though you have given them ample opportunity to do so. You can model non-judgemental feedback by saying something like: 'We are two hours into today's training programme, and no one has asked a question or offered an opinion. I'm concerned, because I don't know how well you understand the material that has

been presented. As a result, I feel anxious – separate from you as a group, and very much alone.'

Obviously, you will have to process what you just said. But participant learning will occur because you were able to model the behaviour taught by applying it in the classroom situation.

Usually it is easier to model single rather than groups of behaviours. For instance, it is simpler to model a non-judgemental feedback statement than it is to model the nine key behaviours in conducting a performance appraisal (complete with 49 sub-behaviours).

2   Another modelling method is to ask the participants to model a behaviour. The payoff is that the participants can see that other group members can do it; and they also become more involved in the training session. The problem here is that there is risk for the participants who act as models. Therefore, if you elect to use this strategy, ask for (and only accept) volunteers. And, as indicated above, ask the participant(s) to model only single – not sets – of behaviours.

3   The third method, video-modelling tapes, is useful in demonstrating more complex behaviours. There are two main ways of using video-modelling tapes: as negative, and positive, models.

Sometimes the subject matter being taught requires that the participants learn all of the things they should NOT do. For example, if you are teaching a class on 'One-On-One Training Skills', then you might well choose to show a negative video model of common errors made in on-the-job training, including such behaviours as a trainer saying, 'This job is really simple; you'll catch on in no time', or giving too much information at one time to an employee. Errors such as these don't intentionally appear in a positive model. But they do occur on the job, and therefore need to be discussed by the participants. Using negative models of training mistakes can be especially interesting – and fun.

Positive modelling videotapes may be used in several ways. For example, you can teach all of the behaviours using overhead transparencies, or flip charts, and than show a videotape modelling these behaviours. Or you may elect to teach only a sub-section of the content followed by showing just that portion of the video, and then discussing what the group observed. Then you would teach the next sub-section, show that part of the video, followed by discussion – until all of the sub-sections have been covered.

It is also possible to make – or purchase – video modelling tapes that do not have sub-titles (called 'fonts'). This format can be used well with more experienced participants, by showing the modelling tape and then having the participants discover, through subgroup workshops, the key behaviours that were modelled.

Role play

After we teach our group a set of behaviours by 'telling' and 'showing', we must give our participants an opportunity to practise what they have been taught. But role play takes a great deal of time! Over and over again we see quantity substituted for quality, and trainers who ought to know better, 'telling' and 'showing', but not giving their participants the opportunity to actually DO what is being taught.

My advice to you is this: design into your programme the time needed for participant practice. Don't destroy the quality of your training efforts by short-cutting the time needed for applying the information you have provided for your participants. A role play session, made up of four participants per group, will take at least an hour. But it is time well spent. The participants learn from each other, gain confidence in their ability to actually use what is taught – and often see the practice session as the highlight of the training day.

When designing role play into your programme, you need to first give the participants an opportunity to prepare for the role play. They will need time to become familiar with the content of the role play case they will use, work out how they will apply to the case the behaviours they were taught, and to make any notes they will need to use during the practice session. As an example, a transparency for preparing your subgroups for a 'One-On-One Training Skills' role play session might look like that in Figure 10.

When the participants have finished their preparation, call time and give the general role play instructions. Again, using the preceding example, the transparency in Figure 11 is an illustration of how the instructions can be given.

At this point, it is usually best to provide more specific instructions to the 'observers' and other participants in the practice session before they

---

PREPARATION FOR PRACTICE

– USING THE TASK EARLIER DETAILED, LOCATE AND COMPLETE THE TRAINING PREPARATION WORKSHEET FORM FOUND IN YOUR HANDOUTS (PAGE 17) ON ONE OF THE DETAILED TASKS.

– SELECT A SMALL TASK THAT CAN BE TAUGHT IN 10 MINUTES OR LESS.

– PREPARE ANY TEACHING AIDS THAT MAY BE REQUIRED.

– DO NOT START THE ACTUAL TRAINING UNTIL YOU RECEIVE ADDITIONAL INSTRUCTIONS.

– 15 MINUTES' TIME WILL BE ALLOWED FOR PREPARATION.

Figure 10   Visual 1

PRACTICE SESSION

1   IN TEAMS OF FOUR, DETERMINE WHO WILL TEACH WHOM FIRST.

2   ONE OBSERVER SHOULD BE A RUTHLESS TIMEKEEPER. THERE IS A MAXIMUM OF ONLY 15 MINUTES TRAINING TIME PER PERSON.

  – ROLE PLAY: 10 MINUTES
  – OBSERVER'S FEEDBACK AND DISCUSSION: 5 MINUTES

3   OBSERVERS WILL MAKE WRITTEN NOTES DURING THE ROLE PLAY, AND THESE WORKSHEETS WILL BE PASSED DIRECTLY TO THE 'TRAINER' AFTER THE DISCUSSION.

4   ROTATE ROLES UNTIL ALL PARTICIPANTS IN YOUR TEAM HAVE HAD AN OPPORTUNITY TO BE AN OBSERVER, TRAINEE AND TRAINER.

Figure 11   Visual 2

begin the actual role play. Continuing with the same example, the observers' instruction might be presented as shown in Figure 12.

For more difficult or longer role plays, you may also need to supply specific instructions to the role playing partners as in Figure 13.

OBSERVERS:

1   FIRST, ASK THE 'TRAINER' WHAT HE OR SHE LIKED ABOUT WHAT WAS DONE, AS WELL AS WHAT THEY WOULD CHANGE.

2   COMMENTS SHOULD BE MADE ON HOW WELL THE TRAINER USED THE STEPS IN TRAINING, NOT ON WHAT TASK WAS TAUGHT.

3   TWO POSITIVE COMMENTS MUST BE MADE BY THE OBSERVERS FOR EACH AREA OF NEEDED IMPROVEMENT MENTIONED.

4   WHEN PROVIDING FEEDBACK TO THE TRAINER ON AREAS THAT MAY NEED IMPROVEMENT, AVOID BEING JUDGEMENTAL. SIMPLY STATE WHAT YOU OBSERVED, IN TERMS OF BEHAVIOURS – OR THEIR ABSENCE.

5   I WILL NOT SEE YOUR OBSERVER WORKSHEETS. THEY WILL BE PASSED DIRECTLY TO THE 'TRAINER'.

6   LOOK FOR:

  – EARLY USE OF TRAINING OUTLINE AND OBJECTIVES WITH THE TRAINEE
  – EARLY USE OF QUESTIONS TO GAIN KNOWLEDGE FROM THE TRAINEE
  – LISTENING SKILLS (NO INTERRUPTIONS)
  – APPROPRIATE EXPLANATION (NOT TOO MUCH AT ONE TIME)
  – DEMONSTRATION WITH VERBAL INSTRUCTIONS THROUGHOUT
  – GUIDANCE CLUES BY TRAINER AS TRAINEE PERFORMS
  – POSITIVE FEEDBACK BY TRAINER TO TRAINEE WHEN THE TASK IS DONE SUCCESSFULLY.

Figure 12   Visual 3

> **INSTRUCTIONS TO THE 'TRAINEE':**
>
> 1 DO NOT BE OBSTINATE OR UNDULY DIFFICULT IN THE PRACTICE SESSION. YOUR 'TRAINER' IS TRYING TO LEARN AND PRACTISE A SET OF KEY BEHAVIOURS, NOT DEAL WITH A PROBLEM EMPLOYEE.
>
> 2 IF YOU ARE ASKED QUESTIONS BY YOUR TRAINER, PROVIDE REASONABLE RESPONSES IF POSSIBLE, (THE WORD IS 'REASONABLE', NOT NECESSARILY 'REALISTIC').
>
> 3 PLEASE STAY IN CHARACTER IN THE ROLE PLAY. DO NOT 'HAM IT UP' FOR THE BENEFIT OF YOUR OBSERVERS. NATURAL HUMOUR IS OK. BUT DON'T TRY TO BE FUNNY, AS IT MAKES IT DIFFICULT FOR YOUR TRAINER.
>
> 4 BE PREPARED ALSO TO PROVIDE FEEDBACK TO YOUR TRAINER AT THE CONCLUSION OF THE ROLE PLAY.

Figure 13   Visual 4

Note how generic the one-on-one training example in Figure 13 is. With each of the four transparencies you could change the word 'Trainer' to 'Manager' and 'Trainee' to 'Employee', and have the structure for facilitating a performance appraisal, coaching and counselling, delegation or interviewing and selecting role play.

If you do use role play in your sessions, let the participants know early in the programme that practice time will be provided. Briefly mention that the role play will be as 'low risk' as you can make it and that no one will be deliberately embarrassed. If you plan to have the participants practise at their individual tables rather than in front of everybody, then tell them so. Some participants will have had quite miserable experiences with role play in the past, and may be feeling some anxiety about what will happen. Try to reduce this anxiety as much as possible, since too much anxiety interferes with good learning.

Games

When we speak of 'games', we are not referring to the more formalized, often computer-based, strategies that are used to teach management decision-making. Games, as discussed here, refers to other structured learning experiences that are described by Webster as, 'any form of play or way of playing' – and, we will add, that have positive learning outcomes for our participants.

Games allow us to help participants examine their own values, knowledge or behaviours by simulating reality in the classroom – and at the same time to have fun! Unfortunately, what participants *think* they do on the job and what they really do are often two very different things. But games can help them experience what is real for them, and, if the game is processed at its conclusion, gain new awareness of themselves.

There is a wide variety of games which can be used, and they may be roughly categorized as follows:

- **'Ice breakers' – e.g., exercises used at the beginning of a programme to help the participants develop group cohesion, and reduce anxiety:**
  Example: There are numerous variations of the 'Name Game'. One example of this game is to ask a participant to give his or her first name. The next participant gives his or her own name, along with the name of the first participant. This continues around the room until it reaches the facilitator, who has to remember everyone's name – as well as add a one-word description of himself or herself. Then, going around the room again, each participant in turn gives the name of all the participants who preceded him or her, in addition giving the one-word descriptor of each of the participants. If someone forgets, one of the other participants may help out.

  This game is an excellent way to help the participants get to know each other better, and to begin to establish connections between themselves.

- **Games that introduce and demonstrate the need for a topic:**
  Example: The following old and interesting game is used to teach the principle that it is usually easier to do a job if you have a set of general guidelines to follow. (I have seen it used as a lead-in to teaching behavioural modelling programmes like Performance Appraisal or One-On-One Training.)

  Write the numbers 1 to 50, at random, on a sheet of A4-sized paper. The numbers are not placed in rows horizontally across the sheet, and are tilted at various angles to each other.

  The facilitator then has the participants individually locate the number '1', then '2' and so forth – locating as many numbers as possible in 40 seconds. After calling time, the facilitator records the highest number reached by each of the participants.

  The facilitator next discusses the patterns, or general guidelines, of the number game: e.g., each number is tilted to point to the next higher number, the smaller numbers are toward the centre, and so forth.

  After discussing these patterns, the participants are given an opportunity, now knowing the guidelines, to repeat the exercise. The average scores will be significantly better. Last, the facilitator asks, 'If you knew in advance the patterns to use in … (conducting a performance appraisal, etc.), do you feel you might be more effective?' After the participants respond in the affirmative, the trainer then proceeds to teach the topic's behaviours.

- **Games as an alternative way of teaching a topic:**

  Example: Your imagination is the limit here. Let's make one up now. We'll call our game, 'Factual Pursuit'. Prepare a number of cards with questions based on your programme's content. (Remember, the questions are on the programme's content with has NOT yet been taught.) Each subgroup is dealt five cards by the facilitator. The participants in each subgroup quietly discuss (so the other groups can't hear) the questions they were dealt, and select those question cards which they believe they know the answer to and think the other tables don't. Each table then discards two of their easier five cards, passing them on to the next table (and they will get two cards from another table).

  When the groups have finished discussing their card and passing two of their cards to the next table, each table in rotation asks its first question. The first participant at another table who knows the question says, 'Answer!' if that person correctly answers the question, his or her table receives one point. (The facilitator has the answers to the questions and is the judge.) If no one at another table knows the answer, or if the participant who said 'Answer!' got it wrong, then the table that asked the question must answer it. If that table gives the correct answer, they get one point. If they get it wrong, they lose a point. The game continues until all questions have been asked and answered.

  Having just now made this game up, I am not sure how long this game will take (I would guess one hour). The time may be increased or decreased simply by increasing or decreasing the number of cards that are passed out to each subgroup.

  The point of this game is this: any trainer, given time, can come up with fun ways to teach a subject! We don't always have to use transparencies or flip charts.

- **Games that provide experiential evidence:**

  Example: 'The Instruction Game', by Training House.

  The games developed over the years by Training House are among the cleverest available. This particular game is designed to teach the principle that new knowledge is best learned by 'hanging it on the hooks of old experience'. In

'The Instruction Game', you divide the participants into two groups. Each group gets a different, but statistically equal, numerical code that will be taught to the other group. After preparing (learning the code and working out how it should be taught), the groups pair up one-on-one, and teach each other their codes. The secret, which the participants don't discover until after they process at the end, is that the individuals who think of using a 'clock' analogy to teach the code do significantly better than those who don't.

I have used this game hundreds of times, and it has never failed to produce an 'Ah-ha!' type of experience for the participants.

- **Games which review and summarize portions of a programme:**
  Example: A popular game used by many trainers is a variation of 'Noughts and Crosses'. Suppose that you are teaching a group of trainers how to use the overhead projector. You have presented the concepts, discussed them and given each participant an opportunity to practise. You then review the material by using this game. For example, you can write on 3" × 5" cards 20 short-answer questions about the overhead projector:
    - If you are right-handed, on which side of the room does the projector screen go (facing towards the participants)?
    - When using the overhead projector, it is best to dim the room lights. 'True' or 'False'?

  Then draw a 'Noughts and Crosses' grid on a sheet of transparency film and project the image on the screen. Divide the participants into two teams, have each team elect a leader, and then give ten of the question cards to each team. Next, flip a coin and ask one team to call it for their choice of 'X' or 'O' (the 'O' team will ask the first question). Each team quietly discusses and selects the questions they think are the most difficult, and orders them from most difficult to least difficult. Then the facilitator calls 'Time', and the 'O' team reads aloud their first most difficult question to the 'X' team. If the 'X' team answers the question correctly, the leader of the 'X' team places an 'X' mark on the Noughts and Crosses grid, and they receive another question from the 'O' team. If the 'X' team answers the question incorrectly (as judged by the facilitator, who supplies the correct answer), they lose their turn and the 'O' team is asked a question selected by the 'X' team. The first team to place three 'Xs' or 'Os' in a row is the winner.

- **Games applying knowledge already taught:**
  Example: It has been a long day. You have presented to your group

nine key steps in conducting a performance appraisal, and discussed each step in detail. You showed an excellent modelling tape that depicted a manager conducting a performance appraisal with her supervisor, and led a good discussion of the things the manager did well and the things the group felt the manager could have improved.

Now it is time for application. But successfully role playing nine key steps (and over 100 sub-steps) in one role play will be difficult for the participants. Therefore, during your initial planning for this workshop you decided to use a game to help them practise the various key steps (and sub-steps) before asking them to role play the entire performance appraisal process.

So you wrote out role play questions based on the behaviours to be taught, such as the ones below:

- The employee says, 'I'll just have to try harder.' You responded by saying ...
- The first thing you do in greeting the employee when he or she walks into your office or the conference room is ...
- You have carefully analysed the reason for your employee's performance problem, and you both feel that you have determined the most probable cause of the difficulty. The next thing you should do is ...

Write 30 to 40 such role play questions (try to have at least two for each participant). Each question and response will take about one to two minutes of classroom time.

To begin the game, you may use normal subgrouping (four or five participants per table), and have each team elect a leader. Then you read one question to each of the subgroups in rotation, allowing them a maximum of 30 seconds to discuss the statement and arrive at their response (you keep time). The leader assigns someone at his or her table to stand up and act out the correct response. (The individuals at each table will rotate in role playing.) You act as the judge, recording on flip chart paper one point for each correct answer. (An entertaining variation is to let the next team act as the judge – with you as the arbiter on any disagreements.) The game is over when you have read all of the questions, and the winner is the team that has the most correct responses.

One word of advice. Don't use games simply for their entertainment value. Games should clearly meet your training objectives, and be used as interesting alternative ways of teaching your participants the programme content. Thus, games need to be processed at their conclusion. Discuss with the group what happened in the game, and what they have learned. In addition, since games create awareness, rather than producing future plans, you should discuss with the participants what they intend to DO with what they have learned.

Training media

There are many types of media available for trainers today. Among them are several we will not attempt to examine: sound/slide presentations; 35 mm. film strips; 16 mm. films; opaque projectors; in-basket exercises; programmed instruction; and simulations. These media formats are either out of date (35 mm. film strips), have been superseded by more popular media (video has replaced 16 mm. film in this country), or are highly specialized (e.g., in-basket exercises and programmed instruction). Instead, we will concentrate on five more popular types of media available today.

Handouts

I am a firm believer in handouts! They allow participants to focus on learning, rather than on taking notes. And if you use overhead transparencies or flip charts to present programme content, then handouts are a must. The main problem (but also important advantage) in using transparencies is that you can present information very quickly – much faster than anyone can possibly write. Thus, providing handouts prevents participants from becoming frustrated by frantically trying to copy down the information being presented. Handouts also enable participants to better utilize the information back on the job by serving as memory aids.

An effective design strategy here is to first prepare a rough draft of your participant handouts by using the planning process presented earlier for selecting the programme's content (pages 7–27). Then, determine the best training strategies for teaching the content of your programme. This will help determine what worksheets or forms may be needed for inclusion in the handouts (observer worksheets, cases, role play instructions, etc.).

Because it may take 10 to 20 or more pages of handout material to properly cover a one-day programme, it is usually best to collate and assemble them by stapling, or use some form of binding. And don't print both sides of the handout pages. By leaving one side of each page blank (or lined), the participant will be able to use that space for taking additional notes that are needed or desired.

People the world over tend to judge a product's quality by the way it is 'packaged'. And this is also true for training material. Participants will experience the training processes you select; but they SEE the media. They observe the quality of the videotapes, the overhead transparencies and participant's manuals, and this, unfortunately or not, influences their judgement about the programme's content. Your content might be outstanding. But if you have poorly prepared transparencies and handouts, full of typing errors and misspellings, your content will be negatively evaluated by some before you even have a chance to present them.

Decide to spend what is necessary to have presentable handouts. Typeset them if possible. Print them on 100 gsm white cartridge paper. Use two-ring binders – either silkscreened (more expensive and normally used when quantities are large), or with clear view covers that will accept preprinted inserts. Utilize indexes and tabs, number the pages for easy reference and include a bibliography for those participants who take charge of their own learning. In short, you want your participants to say: 'Wow! Are these ours to keep?'

When the participants are using their handouts, either in the workshop or outside of it, they appreciate it if they are easy to read. Use short sentences. Avoid using our HRD 'jargon' like the plague! And most important: write like you speak. Most of us are much better writers than we imagine – if we can forget some of the self-consciousness and negative self-perceptions many of us have experienced from the time we entered school.

For example: because I was born dyslexic, I always thought that I was a terrible writer. I can't spell. I mix up lower case 'bs' and 'ds', and even write my '2s' backwards on occasion. And I failed the sixth grade at Beverley Manor Elementary School in Staunton, Virginia.

So my natural conclusion was that I couldn't write. Fortunately, I met a remarkable teacher – Dr Bill Griffin, a professor of English at Virginia Commonwealth University. After looking at an article I had written, Bill said, 'Dick, you are a wonderful writer! You've learned the secret of writing like you talk.' Was that an exciting day for me! That was some 25 years ago, and since that time I have written thousands of pages of training manuals, many articles and even a book.

Don't misunderstand me. I still need the help of a proofreader, since my spelling, grammar and syntax are still awful. But I'm not afraid to write! I'm not afraid of being me as I write for you. And the end result, I have been told by many, is more than adequate.

If you feel that writing is hard or that you lack ability to write well, get some help with the MECHANICS of writing. But if you write like you talk – and you must be a fairly effective speaker or you wouldn't be a trainer – you will likely be a good writer.

Prepared flip charts

Usually, flip charts are used to capture participants' ideas, either when they are doing subgroup work or you are leading a discussion. But flip charts can also be prepared in advance of a workshop and used as an alternative to overhead transparencies. You might select flip charts:

- as a way of keeping information before your group during a programme. For example, if you are teaching a seminar on 'Goal Setting', you might choose to write the key steps on a flip chart in advance of the session. These key steps will then be visible to the participants during the programme, allowing them to see the entire goal-setting process while you present each of the steps in more detail using overhead transparencies.
- if you don't have access to the equipment or materials to make and/or project quality overhead transparencies.
- to mix your media for variety of presentation.

And when preparing flip charts, use dark (black, brown or dark blue, but NOT red), wide-tipped magic markers. And when you print, use all upper case letters ('abc' = lower case, 'ABC' = upper case). Words made with dark markers and upper case letters are much easier for participants to read, especially those seated at the back of the room.

When you buy flip chart paper, try to get paper that has feint ruled lines already printed on the paper. This will help you print professional-looking letters (the participants will not be able to see the ruled lines). You can even print, with light pencil, your own notes in the margin of the flip chart paper. You will be able to see the notes, though the participants will not.

Transparencies

I have used overhead transparencies to facilitate group training for many years. I always had the feeling that I had more effective sessions when I used them. Then the Wharton School of Business and the 3M Company conducted an interesting study that supported what I had intuitively believed. They asked 136 Master's degree candidates to conduct 36 meetings for the purpose of introducing a new 'product', 'Crystal Beer'. The case for Crystal Beer was cleverly written so that the reasons for and against accepting the product were statistically even. The variable in the study was the method of presentation – overhead transparencies vs. whiteboard. (A whiteboard is a state-of-the-art blackboard. It has a white, glossy finish, and can be written on using dry magic markers in a variety of colours.) The meetings and their outcomes are listed in the following table:

Number of meetings	Position	Presentation method	Outcome
12	Pro Crystal Beer	Overheads	67% – 'Go with the beer.'
	Con Crystal Beer	Whiteboard	33% – 'No beer.'
12	Pro Crystal Beer	Whiteboard	33% – 'Go with the beer.'
	Con Crystal Beer	Overheads	67% – 'No beer.'
12	Pro Crystal Beer	Whiteboard	50% – 'Go with the beer.'
	Con Crystal Beer	Whiteboard	50% – 'No beer.'

As the results indicate, the use of overhead transparencies had a positive impact on the subjects' decisions. Even more interesting was that the audience perceived the presenters who used transparencies as being more professional, persuasive, credible, interesting and better prepared. The researchers also found that the whiteboard resulted in presentations that tended to be monologues; while the overhead transparencies produced more group discussion. Last, the meetings that were conducted using overhead transparencies were much shorter because the groups made their decisions faster. For all these reasons, transparencies are the medium of choice for most professional trainers today.

Transparency construction

Making transparencies can be fun! All the required materials are available locally in a wide selection of films and colours. First, there are two main categories of film – dry copy and infra-red. Dry copy film makes transparencies using a regular electrostatic plain-paper copier. Here an image is created on the transparency film in the same way you would make a normal plain-paper copy. The film is loaded in the paper holder of the copy machine, a black and white original is placed under the mat and the result is a printed film.

This method will produce only a black image on a clear or coloured (red, blue, green or yellow) background. Because the transparency film has a slightly 'greasy' finish, the transparency images are not as sharp as those on infra-red film. And because the plain-paper copier will produce only a black image, many users prefer the infra-red method.

Several companies produce an infra-red, desktop transparency machine. But if you can 'beg, borrow or buy' a used 3M Thermofax infra-red desktop copier, do so! If you happen to own one, dig it out. Because of the unappealing yellowish paper copies they make, these once-popular copiers were relegated to the back closet. But they can be used to make outstanding transparencies either with a black image on a clear or coloured background, or with coloured images on clear background. Several companies offer locally available film that can be used with this copier, which will produce red, green, blue and violet images from a black-and-white paper master, adding great variety to your transparencies.

Felt-tip permanent pens for use on transparencies can also be purchased in a variety of colours and tip widths. These can be used to highlight key statements or to box in an important paragraph. But make sure that your pens are of the PERMANENT type. 'Temporary' pens will smear badly, destroying the appearance of a finished transparency.

Rub-on numbers, letters and symbols can be obtained to enhance your visual, and result in transparencies that are easily read. Make sure to use upper case letters, since lower case letters are difficult to read. And one word of caution: don't put your rub-on's on a master and then try to run it through a desktop transparency maker. The heat may cause the letters to lift off the master and stick to the film. Instead, either apply the rub-on directly to the finished film; or make a paper copy of your master and use the resultant COPY to produce the transparency.

In addition, the professional paper masters can be produced by any typesetter at most well-equipped print shops. The only problem is cost. Typeset work is expensive. But if you have the budget, it is considerably easier to have a typesetter lay out and set your masters than to try to make them yourself using rub-on's or the Kroy/3M machine. Just hand print or type your 'visual' on an $8\frac{1}{2}$" × 11" sheet of paper, and take it to a print shop to be typeset. Be sure to also take a transparency frame of the size you plan to use so that the type can be set clearly within the margins of the frame. A 'Helvetica' type with a font size of not less than 16 point and larger point size headings (20–36 point), depending on the amount of information, will result in clear, professional transparencies.

Computer desktop publishing systems can also be used to create paper masters for transparency production. However, the need for large, smooth-edge letters will require a laser printer which usually increases the initial programme cost. In addition, learning to use a desktop publishing programme requires a considerable investment of time.

And do frame your transparencies. Frames make handling your transparencies easier, and also allow you space to write 'cheat notes' on the margins. This will free you from the leader's guide, and allow you to make better, more consistent eye contact with the participants. Frames also allow you to make horizontally lettered transparencies, since the frame will mask the light that would normally spill out of the top and bottom.

This discussion is not complete without mentioning the two main problems in designing transparencies: 1) trying to put too much on one transparency; and, 2) using print that is too small to be read by the participants. The first is confusing. And the second is frustrating, especially to those seated toward the back of the room.

When making transparency paper masters, use the 'KISS' formula: 'Keep it simple, stupid!' Usually, '6 × 6' is a good rule of thumb – a maximum of six words across and six lines down will keep your transparencies from being too 'busy'. Transparencies are used to illustrate key points or serve as outlines, and don't require the programme's complete content. The '6 × 6' rule is only a guideline, however. If, for example, you want to present complete instructions to your participants for a role play exercise, you may create a very detailed transparency that can contain over one hundred words.

Transparency design

There are two kinds of transparencies: 'content' and 'process'. Content transparencies present the programme's concepts and ideas, and process transparencies are used to give group instructions, as shown in Figure 14.

Content and process transparencies are excellent for both you, the trainer and the participants. They reduce your preparation time by serving as visible outlines during the programme. In addition, they also make it easier to maintain eye contact with the participants while presenting the programme's information. They also enable you to increase the amount of information that can be presented in a given period of time. Last, using transparencies makes it easier for a new trainer to lead a high quality workshop – so much so, in fact, that even your line managers can look like 'heroes' to their own people if you wish to train them as trainers.

But the most important reasons for using transparencies have nothing to do with us as trainers. The main reasons for using them are to improve

Example of a content transparency	Example of a process transparency
THE PROBABILITY OF EMPLOYEE SUCCESS TENDS TO INCREASE AS WE: – EXPECT SUCCESS – PROVIDE MEANINGFUL TRAINING – GIVE EXTRINSIC FEEDBACK – REDUCE TENSION **AND THE TRAINEE** – KNOWS HE/SHE CAN MASTER THE JOB – PERCEIVES EXTERNAL REWARDS – RECEIVES INTRINSIC FEEDBACK **AND** – PEER GROUP PRESSURE IS POSITIVE – MANAGEMENT SUPPORTS OUR EFFORTS	1 ELECT LEADERS AT EACH TABLE 2 WRITE COMMENTS DIRECTLY ON YOUR GROUP'S FLIP CHART PAPER 3 ANSWER THE FOLLOWING QUESTIONS: – WHAT ARE YOUR EXPECTATIONS? – WHAT ARE YOUR RESERVATIONS? 4 REPORT YOUR GROUP'S COMMENTS ANONYMOUSLY

Figure 14   Transparency design examples

participant retention of the programme's ideas and concepts, make it much easier for participants to remember their group's instructions and to reduce the chance of misunderstanding.

I freely admit I am strongly biased toward using overhead transparencies. And I know there are a few trainers who are just as strongly biased against them. If you happen to fall into the latter category, you can, of course, use flip charts.

Audio recordings

To the surprise of some trainers, audio recordings are a very good training tool – if properly used. They may be used in place of a MUCH more expensive videotape, or to add variety to your training programme or as an inexpensive way to conduct simultaneous role plays with a number of subgroups.

Many years ago I was asked to conduct a basic selling skills training programme for new salespeople. Since I already had an outstanding generic selling skills programme, and as a result wouldn't need to spend much development time on the project, I told the client that I would do it. As always, I spent several weeks riding around with experienced and new salespeople – while they sold farm supplies to farmers. One of the main differences I found between the high sales producers and the low ones was the former group's ability to 'close' the sale.

It quickly became apparent that it was important for the salespeople to have a close rapport with their customers. And most of them did – for the majority of the salespeople had been hired originally because of their farming background, and were even related to other farmers in the area. But because of their close relationship to their customers, many of the salespeople felt that it somehow wasn't appropriate to 'ask for the business'. 'When they're ready to buy,' they said, 'they will call.'

But too frequently they didn't call. And in the meantime a new competitive sales force had entered their market area and was gaining substantial sales volume.

Obviously, one of the key topics I needed to present to this organization was the concept of closing – tactfully and with integrity – on their call objective. One of the senior salespeople whom I spent time with was consistently a volume and profit producer. And what a closer! It was simply a pleasure watching him sell. I asked him how he felt about using closing techniques on his clients. He replied, 'My job is to make it easy for them to buy – and a good close does just that.' 'How,' I asked, 'do you think your clients feel about someone using closing techniques on them?' 'Well,' he replied, 'if I've done my job in finding out what they really need, and have presented my product and service in its best possible light, then they like me to close. They *want* me to close.'

I could have made a videotape of that interview – for about $5,000! Instead, I put this master salesman's message on audio tape, word for word, and used it as the introduction to the closing section of my selling skills sessions. And it worked wonders! The total cost? Five dollars for the audio tape, and my time.

If you decide to use an audio recording in a programme, make sure that the playback unit you select has large enough speakers to be easily heard throughout the room. Even smaller tape recorders often permit external speaker jacks which can be used with large speakers to ensure good audio quality.

Another way of using audio tape is as a low cost substitute for video in simultaneous role plays. Simply provide an audio recorder for each subgroup which can record their role play at their own table. Of course, it will require extra time for the participants to listen to and critique the audio tape – approximately $1\frac{1}{2}$ hours for a subgroup of four or five participants. But the discussion and feedback will be more accurate than in using observers without a recording device.

Video recordings

First, a 'word to the wise' about making your own video modelling tapes. In most cases – don't! Unless you are fortunate enough to have your own in-house studio, complete with multiple cameras, lights and lighting crews, live switching, graphics generator, quality recorders, tight scripts and COMPETENT actors, the chances are that the videotape you end up with will not meet your own standards of quality. We have raised a generation of very sophisticated TV-watchers who know what good video is – and is not. And a poor video is very easy to make!

Making your own videos

For several years, I hired competent actors to act as the 'narrator' in our video productions. Then one day, after watching Peter Drucker serve as his own narrator in an excellent videotape, I said, 'If he can do it, I can do it.' Was I wrong! As a narrator, I was a 'bad actor'. And it cost me considerable money to remake the video with a professional actor as narrator.

As a rule of thumb, if you are committed to making your own videotape, hire professional TALENT! You can almost always hire better actors than you can 'home grow'. And it was remarkably little to do with how photogenic your people may 'look' to you. My wife says I look pretty good 'for an old guy' – even kind of distinguished with grey in my beard, most of my hair on top, and wearing a conservative suit with silk tie (softly understated) and a French cuff shirt. But I often don't come across well on camera. And, in my opinion, few people do!

If you have to make your own video and you have never done it before, you will need some help. You can call another trainer who you know has done video and get his or her advice. Or you can contract local video production houses. If you plan to use an outside production house, then talk to several different ones. You will find them very helpful in planning your video production.

Generally, the steps in producing a quality videotape are:

1   Research the content. Determine exactly what behaviours you want the videotape to model.
2   Write the script (or have it written). Writing a script is hard work. It is not the same as writing a journal article or creating a participant's manual. It requires the ability to write like people really speak. For example, if I were to rewrite this paragraph as a script, it might look something like this:

Narrator: 'Let me give you a piece of advice. Don't even think about writing your own script. Oh, I know, we're all great writers – especially you and me. And writing a script sounds so simple. But it's a whole lot harder to do than it looks.

Now you know that we've all learned to talk to people. And we've learned to write to people. But few of us have learned to write like we talk to people. And that's exactly what you are going to have to do – if you MUST write your own script!'

If you do decide to write your own script, try to make the script as generic as possible. Jobs change, procedures change – and even language changes. You don't want a future participant to think, right in the middle of your video, 'Hey, that's an old procedure' – and totally miss the key behaviour that is being appropriately modelled at that moment.

Secondly, don't make the frequent mistake of writing a script that is too long. Twenty minutes of video is about all most participants can process at any one time. If your video is longer than that, the chances are that you need to be more succinct.

3   Hire the very best actors you can afford. (Outstanding actors can make even a poor script look acceptable.) Consider using local actors. Bringing in 'talent' from Hollywood can get a bit expensive – unless of course, you live in such an area. Most local video actors make their living doing commercials in order to do what they really want – local theatre, or a production like yours. So you will usually find them eager to do a good job. In selecting actors, try to remember local television commercials that really stuck in your mind because the acting was unusually good. Then call the organization that makes the product that was being sold and find out who the actors were.

AGAIN: DO NOT USE IN-HOUSE PEOPLE AS ACTORS! Suppose that you got talked into using a couple of your employees as actors for a large video production. Six months later, one of the 'stars' is fired for misappropriation of the organization's funds, and the other has had an affair with another employee and is now facing a charge of sexual harassment. These examples are extreme; but such problems occur. People retire, resign, are demoted, fired and die – and leave you with an outdated video.

When you select your actors, it is important to tell them about the 'two-step rehearsal process' described below (4). This process will take more of their time and they will need to charge you a bit more for the job. Also state that 'teleprompters' will not be allowed. (Don't let anyone talk you into using a teleprompter. They make for awful acting!)

Select actors that HAVE HAD VIDEO EXPERIENCE, not just live audience stage work. Most good actors will have videotapes of their past work. Ask to see them!

If you need a narrator, don't repeat my mistake by trying to do it yourself. And I also suggest that you don't use your chief executive officer as the narrator. Organizational officials not only have a way of fading from the scene, resulting in an outdated video, but are usually, in my experience, poor video actors.

4   Make your final videotape using a 'two-step' process. The first step is to get the script to the actors as early as possible. Ask them to memorize it, and be prepared to suggest slight word changes where appropriate. Then, videotape the first practice session using your own in-house videotape recorder. Watch this rough copy of the practice session six or seven times, and with pen in hand make notes of things that may have looked fine on paper but not on video. Next, call a couple of your most talented HRD friends and show them the practice video, asking for their suggestions and ideas. You will be amazed at the number of changes you decide to make. And some of the changes often concern things that can become disasters if they are not corrected in this first step.

The second step is to call the actors, give them the changes, and ask them to memorize the new script and be prepared to do the final production on the scheduled date.

5   In most cases, don't go out and buy expensive video recording equipment! After you see the results of your first video, you may not use it again.

A far better strategy is to rent what you need for a couple of days. Call around and find out which are the best video production houses in your area. Look for things like full-time camera crews, multiple cameras, live switching capability, lighting crews and one-inch or Beta-Cam recording equipment. If you want a professional video, you are going to need to hire a professional group of people to help you. So hire the production house's studio for the time you need, and let them help you with things like 'sets', blocking out the actors' moves and suggestions for good talent in your area. And at an early point (BEFORE you finalize the script), they are going to need a copy of your script, and some idea of your budget.

It is probably best not to attempt to do a video production 'on site' at your location. It is very hard to control noise (airplanes overhead, air-conditioning, telephones, public address systems and outside traffic), as well as employees at your organization. Most professional studios are soundproofed, and generally do an excellent job of controlling noise.

It is difficult to know how much studio time you will need. For a low-budget, 20-minute videotape, you can count on at least one-half day to set up the studio (install the 'walls' and furniture, set the lighting, place the cameras and so forth), one day for shooting the scenes and another full day for editing the videotape.

Pre-recorded videotapes

Some of the more important criteria for purchasing stand-alone videotapes to use in your programme are shown in the following checklist:

1   Is the topic appropriate for the subject being taught?   ————————

2   Are the ideas presented in the video concurrent with the concepts that are being taught in the programme?————————

3   Is the 'setting' appropriate for your organization?————

4   Does the video appear out of date?
    Dress?————————
    Hairstyles?————————
    Language?————————
    What is the copyright date?   ————————

5   Is the script believable?   ————————

6   Are the actors believable?   ————————

7   How good is the technical quality of the production?   ————————

8   What is the cost of the videotape?
    Preview cost?   ————————
    Rental cost?   ————————
    Purchase cost or licence fees?————————

9   How long can we keep it?   ————————
    Preview (days)   ————————
    Rental (days)————————

Putting it all together

In the last part of Step Nine – 'Selecting Training Strategies, Methods and Media' – we will consider the constraints under which we work, the training strategy needed, the appropriate method, the media available and, finally, how to make decisions about the best way to present our programme's content. What at first appears to be almost overwhelming becomes easier to manage when we examine a typical programme's timeline in terms of the four 'As': 'Ask, Advise, Assimilate and Apply'.

Each of these four stages may require a different training method and media mix. The chart shown in Figure 15 can aid us in the selection of our method and media.

When selecting methods and media for a particular segment of a training programme, use the principles presented earlier to guide you in making your decisions (pages 3–7). For example, suppose that you are going to teach a workshop on 'Oral Communication Skills'. As a part of this programme, you plan to teach the skill of 'paraphrasing' – which some trainers call 'reflective listening'. Using the principle, 'Provide the participant with a variety of learning experiences', along with the chart in Figure 15, you decide to use prepared flip chart pages to teach the concept of paraphrasing. Prior to the session, you carefully block letter the statements (using a DARK coloured magic marker) shown in Figure 16.

Next, since you not only want your participants to 'understand' the concept, but also to actually use it (Principle 6: Provide an opportunity to DO what has been taught), you might then think of using another sheet of flip chart paper to write out some role play instructions. But don't! Remember the principle of variety. Possibly a better idea would be to use a different method and media. You could, for example, type out the role play instructions on a sheet of A4 paper (see Figure 17) , have this sheet duplicated and give a copy of the role play instructions to each participant.

Now that you have designed the teaching processes, you might write your own training outline as shown in Figure 18.

When you teach the next topic, try not to use the same methods or media. For example, it might be appropriate to have the groups develop their own model of what to do in a specific situation, and then use a transparency to show the key steps. Next you might choose to model the behaviour by using a videotape, rather than doing the modelling yourself as you did with the preceding topic. Finally, in the practice session you may choose to use larger subgroups for role play rather than the smaller triads used before.

The main point in the above discussion is to select methods and media that will accomplish your training objectives. Since you normally have several methods and media to select from, vary them during the day so that

STRATEGY —

1. ASK: OBTAIN INFORMATION FROM THE PARTICIPANTS		2. ADVISE: PRESENT INFORMATION TO THE PARTICIPANTS		3. ASSIMILATE: PARTICIPANTS PROCESS THE INFORMATION		4. APPLY: PARTICIPANTS UTILIZE THE INFORMATION	
Method	**Media**	**Method**	**Media**	**Method**	**Media**	**Method**	**Media**
Discussion	– Blank easel paper – Blank transparency film – Blackboard or dry marker whiteboard	Presentation	– Prepared flip charts – Video recordings – Transparencies – Handouts	General Discussion	– Prepared flip charts – Transparencies – Handouts	Role play	– Video recording equipment – Work sheet handouts – Audio recording equipment
Buzz Groups	Prepared assignment presented by: – Flip charts – Transparencies – Handouts	General Discussion	– Prepared flip charts – Transparencies – Handouts – Games	Buzz Groups	– Blank easel paper – Handouts	Games	– Handouts
Sub groups	Prepared assignment presented by: – Chalk board or whiteboard – Flip charts – Transparencies – Handouts	Modelling	– Pre-recorded videotapes – Prerecorded audio tapes – Trainer acting as a model	Subgroups	– Blank easel paper – Handouts		
Testing	– Handouts	Brainstorming	– Easel paper	Case Studies	– Handouts		
				Games	– Handouts		

Figure 15 Method and media selection chart

PARAPHRASING (REFLECTIVE LISTENING)

1   LISTEN INTENTLY TO WHAT THE OTHER PERSON HAS TO SAY.

2   WHEN THE OTHER PERSON HAS FINISHED SPEAKING, IN YOUR OWN
    WORDS REPEAT WHAT YOU THINK YOU HEARD, AND ASK IF WHAT YOU
    HEARD WAS CORRECT.

    EXAMPLE: 'WHAT I HEAR YOU SAYING IS ...
       (PARAPHRASE WHAT YOU HEARD).
       IS THAT CORRECT?'

3   YOU DON'T NEED TO USE THE SAME 'PRE-' AND 'POST-STATEMENTS' I
    USED. FEEL FREE TO USE YOUR OWN.

  PRE-STATEMENT EXAMPLES:
   'WHAT THAT MEANS TO ME IS ...'
   'I UNDERSTAND YOU TO SAY ...'
   'SO YOU FEEL THAT ...'

  POST-STATEMENT EXAMPLES:
   'DID I UNDERSTAND THAT CORRECTLY?'
   'DID I HEAR YOU CORRECTLY?'

Figure 16   Pre-prepared flip chart

the programme is interesting for the participants. After you select the method that you will use for each topic in the programme, select the appropriate media for that method.

An example of a completed 'Programme Development Worksheet' is shown in Figure 19.

Step 10 – Selecting and designing programme evaluation

The time to think about evaluating your programme is in the beginning – the design stage. It is much too late to conduct a programme, and *then* attempt to put together some sort of evaluation. Whether all you need is a simple evaluation form that your participants fill out at the close of the workshop, or a more formal cost analysis of the return on invested training time, it only makes sense to view evaluation as a part of your up-front training design.

When we examine the issues in evaluation, there are three major factors to consider:

1   Why conduct evaluations? (Who benefits from them?)
2   When should the evaluation occur?
3   What type of evaluation information needs to be obtained?

ROLE PLAY INSTRUCTIONS

1   Form small groups of three. One of your group members will initially be the speaker, another will be the listener and the third will be an observer.

2   Each group member should now think of a personal opinion that he or she feels is important. (Topics might include: divorce, prejudice, narrow-minded people, drinking and driving, drug addiction, gun control and so forth.) The only criterion is that whatever topic you pick, you feel strongly about it.

3   Next, practise the skill of paraphrasing in rotation. Decide who will be the first speaker, listener and observer.

    Speakers: Don't get too carried away and talk too long. Remember that the listener is going to have to rephrase for you the essence of what you say. If you talk too long, this may become an impossible job.

    Listeners: Listen intently to what the speaker is saying. Do not interrupt, either verbally or non-verbally. When the speaker is finished, try to restate what you heard in your own words. Do not say, 'Well what you are TRYING to say is …' Review the pre-statement examples just shown. When you have restated what you heard, ask the speaker if what you heard was correct. If what you heard was not what the speaker felt was said, the speaker should indicate this and repeat his or her initial statement.

    Observers: Don't enter into the conversation. Listen to what the speaker says and how well the listener paraphrases what was said. Then, provide feedback to the listener after he or she has finished paraphrasing.

4   When you have finished the first session, rotate roles and continue until each person has had a chance to play each role.

5   You have a total of 15 minutes for the practice session (or five minutes for each rotation).

6   Call me if you have any problems or questions.

Figure 17   Role play handout

Let's look at each of these factors, starting with the reasons for conducting an evaluation and who benefits from it.

Why conduct evaluations – and who benefits?

Programmes are evaluated for the following reasons:

- Participants' reason:
  1   The participants' learning can be reinforced by providing them with feedback on their performance.

Topic: Paraphrasing

1   Ask if any of the participants have ever heard of the terms 'paraphrasing' or 'reflective listening' (Principle 2 – Involve participants in their own learning). Since the verification interviews indicated that some of the participants already know this listening skill, there is a good chance that someone in the group will give an affirmative answer. If so, ask that individual (or individuals) to state their understanding of the technique. Reinforce any participation.

2   Tape the prepared flip chart paper on the wall, and briefly discuss each of the steps (Principle 7 – Don't just 'tell' them; show them, as well).

3   Ask for someone to volunteer to talk briefly on a subject about which they have a strong opinion (Principle 4 – Relate to the participant's 'real world'). When someone volunteers, ask that individual to talk for approximately one minute on the subject of his or her choice, while you listen. When they are finished talking, paraphrase what you heard and ask the individual if what you heard was correct. Then ask the group if you followed the steps correctly.

4   Pass out the handout that describes the practice session. Ask the participants to individually read it. Then answer any questions they may have and ask them to begin when they are ready. Remind them that they have only 15 minutes time.

5   Call time at the end of 15 minutes, and ask the participants how it went. Ask if anybody has an example in which the speaker said, 'No, that is NOT what I said!' Discuss the group's comments before moving on to the next topic.

6   Pass out the detailed handout on 'Paraphrasing' so the participants will have specific information on the programme's content to use back on the job (Principle 11 – Follow up on the job what has been taught in the classroom).

Figure 18   Training outline

- Trainer's reasons:
    2   Feedback from the participants during a programme can help you take immediate action to make the programme better.
    3   Evaluations at the close of a programme can provide you with feedback to use in improving the quality of future programmes.
    4   Personal feedback will help you become a better facilitator.
    5   Evaluations force you to continually consider the RESULTS of your training, rather than focusing solely on programme activities.
- Training department reasons:
    6   Additional training needs can be uncovered.
    7   The training department can obtain information to use in appraising the trainer's performance.
- Organization's reasons:
    8   Information can be obtained that will help determine if the programme is achieving results, and whether those results are the ones that are desired.

9   To determine if your training is a £5,000 solution to a £3 problem. In other words, are the training results great enough to justify the investment of training time and money?

10   Evaluations might reveal that other problems exist (problems that may have little to do with training) that hinder application of what was taught. This is another way of saying that you misdiagnosed the cause of the problem when you did the initial needs assessment.

When should we conduct evaluations?

There are three times that evaluations can be conducted: 1) evaluations that occur during the programme (within-training evaluation); 2) evaluations conducted at the close of the programme (terminal evaluation); and, 3) evaluations that measure results on the job (post-training evaluation). Each of these evaluation areas requires different design strategies.

Within-training evaluations

Designing, within-training evaluation is fairly simple. It is usually a matter of planning sufficient classroom time to be able to discuss with the participants how they are feeling about the training programme. For example, you could say something like:

OK, let's stop for a moment and talk together about how you are feeling about the programme up to this point. What thoughts do you have?

You can encourage further discussion by asking questions like:

- What do you like best about what we have done?
- What would you like us to do differently?
- What should we do more of? Less of?

When you are successful in obtaining comments from your participants, try not to get defensive. Don't justify, explain or reply at this time. Let as many people in the group comment as is practical, given time considerations, and then sum up their suggestions and ideas. Finally, make any comments of your own.

Terminal evaluations

Conducting terminal evaluations is also fairly straightforward. You can lead a group discussion using the same types of questions shown in the

PROGRAMME DEVELOPMENT WORKSHEET
OBJECTIVE

Given past performance records of an actual employee who works for the leader, each leader in the training session will be able to discuss the employee's strengths.

ASK

1   Ask, 'What would your reaction be if your boss walked up to your desk and said, "Could I see you in my office?"' (Answer: 'What did I do WRONG?')

ADVISE	
Learning points	**Reasons**
1 It is important to discuss an employee's positive performance in a performance appraisal interview.	A Employees tend to continue what they are reinforced for doing. B Increases morale of employees because most employees enjoy being recognized for positive performance.
2 Etc.	

ASSIMILATE

1   Show video modelling tape of leader providing positive reinforcement to an employee.

APPLY

1   Place participants in triads and ask them to pass their role play preparation worksheets to the person on their right.

Figure 19   Programme development worksheet

PROGRAMME DEVELOPMENT WORKSHEET

Methods, strategies and media

2　Then ask, 'Why would you not think, I wonder what I did RIGHT?' (Answer: 'Nobody ever gets called into the boss's office unless they have fouled up!')

3　Ask, 'Does it have to be that way?' (Answer: 'No!')

4　Ask, 'Would it improve the morale of our people if we took every possible opportunity to give them positive feedback?' (Answer: 'Certainly!')

Evidence	Methods, strategies and media
A　Bandura's study showing an average of 250% increase in desired behaviour when the subjects were given positive reinforcement. B　Herzberg's 2nd motivator and 3rd motivator is 'Recognition'.	A　Discuss first point and Bandura's research using an overhead transparency. B　Pass around non-ordered list of Herzberg's satisfiers and ask participants to rank order them as to what makes them personally happy on the job ('1' = most important). Ask them to turn this list over and not look at it when they do the next assignment. Pass out non-ordered list of Herzberg's dissatisfiers and ask the participants to rank the things that make them personally unhappy on the job ('1' = most unhappy). Tally the top five items from both lists on flip chart paper. Show that 'recognition' is usually ranked high on both lists. Show ranking according to Herzberg.

Methods, strategies and media

2　Print the key steps in providing positive feedback on a 4" × 6" card, and pass out at this time.

3　Have participants individually fill out a role play preparation worksheet, detailing something positive they did on the job.

Methods, strategies and media

2　Tell the participants they will role play themselves in the role play. One team member will be an observer; and the other will be their boss, and give positive feedback using the key steps that were discussed.

3　Give specific 'observer' instructions, and instruct the triads on their time constraints.

Figure 19 (concluded)

85

preceding paragraphs. Or you can use a standard evaluation form which is passed out for the participants to complete. (A sample of this type of evaluation form is presented later in this book.)

Post-training evaluations

There are some important reasons for choosing NOT to do a post-training evaluation. (I can't think of any reason for not doing an evaluation during or at the close of a programme!) One reason is cost. Designing and conducting an evaluation that measures the final outcomes of the training can be very expensive – so expensive in terms of just the time required that you may decide against it. Or, it may be difficult to obtain the data needed for measurement. For example, in some cases you may find that there is no 'bench-mark' of past performance against which to compare the programme's success or failure. On the other hand, the data may well exist but retrieving it may be more work than it is worth.

Another problem that can prevent an effective evaluation is that other factors may impact on the people who were trained to such an extent that the evaluation doesn't measure the effects of the training. For example, suppose you conducted a series of coaching workshops that were designed to improve job attendance (reduce absenteeism and tardiness). Unfortunately, two weeks after the final training session the organization announced an impending reduction in the work force – 20 per cent of the labour force! Your evaluation now might appear to show that attendance got worse rather than better as a result of our training.

Even with these problems, it is rare that you cannot conduct some sort of post-training evaluation. And thinking in terms of post-training evaluation will help you keep the important end results, rather than just details of programme activities, in mind during the entire training cycle of needs assessment, design, implementation and evaluation.

Types of evaluative information

You can evaluate your programme by determining: 1) your own reactions; 2) the participants' reactions; 3) the knowledge gained by the participants; 4) the participants' behaviour; and, 5) participant results back on the job.

Your reactions

Although an evaluation conducted by the person who presented a training programme is not always objective or scientific, it is in fact a rich source of information. Most competent trainers are continually looking for ways to make their programmes more effective. During the programme they try new ideas to make what they do even better, and then attempt to evaluate the results of what they did. It is a mental attitude, a willingness to take risks and, on the spur of the moment, to try something new. It is the internal motivation to be the very best that you can be – a genuine desire to be competent.

The problem lies in knowing how to teach a trainer how to do this! There is no step-by-step process that you can follow, and no 'format' that can easily be given. Yet I know that your evaluation of your work is one of the most important ways of obtaining information for future programme modification and improvement.

Part of the answer may be achieved by writing out in advance key questions to think about during the programme. Then reserve time for yourself after the programme to think about what was accomplished and what changes could be made. Then make WRITTEN notes to yourself about what you will do differently the next time.

For example, in advance of the programme you might write out questions like:

- What parts of the programme feel awkward to me? Why?
- What have I learned from my last experience in conducting this programme that can help me be more effective this time?

Then, during the programme make notes to yourself on potential problem areas and ideas for future improvement. Last, as soon as the programme is over – while it is still fresh in your mind – spend an hour or so reviewing your notes, thinking about the best and worst parts of the day, and write out your thoughts concerning future changes.

Participant reactions

You can assess the participants' reactions to the programme by designing a simple evaluation form for the participants to fill out. At the end of my training programmes, it is always 'Critique the programme time.' And while I pack up, the group fills out THE FORM. I might say that these are just 'happiness reports', or 'This isn't an effective evaluation of the programme', and so forth. But inside it's 'I wonder what they're writing!' So, I look at their evaluation forms to find out what they said about ME. And frequently I find what I know are solid suggestions on how the programme might be improved.

A typical evaluation form might look like that shown in Figure 20.

Note that this type of evaluation provides feedback primarily to the trainer and the training department. It is not intended to provide evalua-

---

PROGRAMME EVALUATION

Name of programme ———————————————— Date ——————

Facilitator ————————————————————————————

Your name (optional) ——————————————————————

Your department, division or section ——————————————

Please rate the following aspects of the programme by circling the appropriate number:

		Poor	Average		Excellent
1	Overall reaction to the programme:	1	2	3	4	5
2	How well did the content of the programme meet your needs?	1	2	3	4	5
3	How well did the programme give you information that you can use on the job?	1	2	3	4	5
4	How well was the programme presented?	1	2	3	4	5

What were the strong points of the programme? ——————————
————————————————————————————
————————————————————————————

How could the programme have been improved? ————————————
————————————————————————————
————————————————————————————
————————————————————————————

Figure 20   Programme evaluation form

tive help for the participants or for the organization. In addition, the participants are usually not trained trainers, and so may lack the knowledge needed to give informative suggestions for improvement. Thus, although a typical evaluation form filled out by the participants at the completion of the programme can do a good job of eliciting their reactions, it is not sufficient by itself.

Another way of obtaining evaluative data on a programme and its facilitator is to allow an extra 15 minutes at the close of the programme for simply asking the participants how they feel about the session. As part of your programme design you can write out several questions in advance to assist you in leading such a discussion, for example:

● What did you like best about today's programme?

- What things do you think we could have improved?
- What information that you learned today will be especially useful back on the job?
- Of all the things we covered today, which parts should we have spent more time on?
- Which things should we have spent less time on?

Questions like these will help you to lead a discussion that can yield significant information for you and your training department. Again, however, we note that this type of evaluation doesn't provide much evaluative information for either the participants or the organization.

You can sometimes gain more accurate information on your participants' reactions by conducting one-on-one interviews with them at a later date. Often the close of a workshop is the high spot of the day, and everyone is feeling good – and generous in their evaluations! Thus you may be able to secure more realistic reactions if you give the participants additional time to evaluate for themselves whether or not the experience of the programme was beneficial.

Knowledge gained

The best way to accurately determine the knowledge gained by training participants is to construct a valid and reliable multiple-choice pre-test and post-test. As was discussed earlier in the media section of this workbook, designing a multiple-choice test is not easy. And it is even more difficult to construct two different but equivalent tests for pre- and post-testing.

Here is the way I do it:

1 Using the programme outline, select the main topics that will be taught to the participants.
2 Identify in the participant's manual the specific topics you have selected.
3 For each topic area, write two, or four, multiple-choice questions of relatively equal difficulty using the techniques discussed earlier in this book in the testing section.
4 Using your common sense, separate the questions into two equal groups. That is, try to place the two (or four) questions that you wrote on each topic into the two groups by their degree of difficulty. (It is almost guaranteed that after you pilot the tests, the tests will be shown to be quite unequal; but at least your effort will put you in the ball park!)
5 Evaluate the tests with a group of participants by randomly dividing the group in two, and giving one half the pre-test and the other half the

post-test. Then, after the training is completed, reverse the process and give the post-test to the group that had the pre-test, and vice versa. If the gain in learning indicated by both test combinations is the same, the tests are probably equivalent. But the chances are that they won't be the same. If this is the case, tally up the number of participants who missed each question on both the pre-test and post-test. This will give you some measure of the difficulty level of each of the questions – and will allow you to move questions around until the tests appear to be more equal.

At the same time you are counting the number of missed questions, also eliminate (or completely rewrite) questions that everyone got correct and questions that no one got right. In addition, tally up the number of times each wrong answer was selected for each person. The wrong answers that no one selected may need to be rewritten to make them more plausible.

6   As you have probably guessed, you then will need to repeat step 5 again with the new version of the pre-test and post-test. If after this they are still not equivalent, you need to repeat this process until they are.

As you can see, designing pre-tests and post-tests is not easy. Thus some trainers prefer to use a special type of perception instrument. This instrument is administered at the end of the programme, and asks the participants to individually rate their knowledge or skill level prior to the session and then to compare this with their present knowledge or skill on the same topics. For example, an evaluation conducted on a 'Performance Appraisal' programme might look like that in Figure 21.

This form needs to be customized for each programme. But if you use the planning process presented in this book, it will be easy to list the specific knowledge and/or behaviours on the form by using the original list that you completed earlier (step 3 of the planning process).

This evaluation strategy still suffers from all of the problems associated with perception instruments. For one, it measures what the participant PERCEIVES is true – not necessarily what IS true! In addition, the results can be influenced by other factors not related to the question of the effectiveness of the programme. For example, the participants may like you as a trainer and want you to look good in the eyes of others who will be evaluating you. Or, if the participants enjoy the opportunity to get away from the job by attending training programmes, they may indicate outstanding results, even if this is not true, in order to ensure that future programmes will be conducted.

Evaluations that attempt to measure knowledge gained can help provide feedback not only to the trainer and the training department, but also to the participants. The participants will be able to give themselves feed-

---

**PERFORMANCE APPRAISAL
PROGRAMME EVALUATION**

Facilitator ———————————————————— Date ——————————

Your name (optional) ————————————————————————————

Your department, division or section ——————————————————

Please indicate in the first column your knowledge or skill level concerning each of the following topics PRIOR to the training programme. Then indicate your PRESENT knowledge or skill level in the second column.

		PRIOR Knowledge or skill				PRESENT Knowledge or skill	
		Low Average High			Low Average High		
1	Completing detailed preparation	1 2 3 4 5			1 2 3 4 5		
2	Filling out the performance appraisal form	1 2 3 4 5			1 2 3 4 5		
3	Preparing the employee for the interview	1 2 3 4 5			1 2 3 4 5		
4	Etc.						

Figure 21   Performance appraisal programme evaluation form

back on how well they learned the material presented. In addition, the pre-test/post-test process can help to motivate them to learn more.

Participant's behaviours

You may evaluate the participant's behaviour in the classroom, and/or on the job. During the training session you can observe the participants' behaviours to determine if in fact they are able to do what they have been taught to do. Prior to the programme, design simple behavioural check-sheets, and fill them out as the participants practise the behaviours. Checksheets which adequately reflect participant behaviours are fairly easy to construct, particularly if you have used the planning process discussed earlier in this book. Obviously, such a form must be programme-specific since it reflects only those behaviours that are taught in that programme. An example of a behavioural checksheet using the 'Performance Appraisal' topic used earlier is shown in Figure 22.

At the end of the programme, you can tally the responses from all of the participants for each behaviour. This will give you a fairly accurate idea of whether or not the participants, as a group, have met your initial training objectives.

**PERFORMANCE APPRAISAL
BEHAVIOURAL CHECKSHEET**

Participant's name _____

Observer _____ Date _____

Indicate the participant's level of skill for each of the behaviours listed below.

Role play behaviour:	Needs improvement	Competent
1 Put the 'employee' at ease.	_____	_____
2 Used words or phrases that were not judgemental.	_____	_____
3 Allowed the 'employee' to do most of the talking.	_____	_____
4 Asked questions to enlist the 'employee's' early involvement in the interview.	_____	_____
5 Brought up areas of concern about the 'employee's' performance.	_____	_____
6 Helped the 'employee' analyse the cause(s) of any performance problems.	_____	_____
7 Probed for 'employee' solutions to any problems discussed.	_____	_____
8 Developed written action plans with the 'employee'.	_____	_____
9 Provided the 'employee' with positive feedback.	_____	_____
10 Discussed the 'employee's' ratings in a non-threatening way.	_____	_____
11 Summarized the interview.	_____	_____
12 Set follow-up dates.	_____	_____

Figure 22   Performance appraisal behavioural checksheet

This form of evaluation also has drawbacks. First, if the individual who conducted the programme is also the one who evaluates the programme, there may well be concern about objectivity. In addition, it is difficult to evaluate participants in the case of multiple role plays. If the participants are role playing at several or more tables at the same time, then it may be necessary to have additional evaluators to observe each table.

You can also, in some cases, obtain evaluations of the participant's behaviour back on the job. In the above example, on-the-job evaluations would be difficult, because it is rare that an evaluator would be able to observe someone conducting a real performance appraisal since they are normally conducted privately. But many other kinds of behaviours can be observed on the job by either you or the leader of the person who was trained. As part of your programme preparation, construct a behavioural checklist (similar to the preceding 'performance appraisal' example). This list can be used by you, or by the leader of the participant who was trained, as an objective way of determining job behaviour.

Participant results on the job

Articles and books on evaluating the job results of a training programme are almost universal in stressing how difficult it is to really determine a programme's return on investment. I disagree! In fact, you can even let your participants do most of the work. Here's how.

1   Reserve time at the end of your programme (approximately 1 hour). Ask your participants to determine all the observable effects that could be indices of organizational efficiency or non-efficiency as a result of the training they received. In advance, make up a transparency or flip chart similar to that in Figure 23 (use examples that fit your organization and training programme).
2   Using this transparency, ask the groups to brainstorm observable effects that fit their specific section, department or individual employees. For example, as a participant I might choose to observe and measure one of my employees who has had an attendance problem – given that the training programme dealt with improving attendance. Or, if I am the leader of a particular section in my organization, I might observe and measure my section's report errors – given the training

---

ON-THE-JOB TRAINING EVALUATION

1   IN TEAMS OF 3–6:

  – ELECT LEADERS OF EACH TEAM
  – USE FLIP CHART PAPER TO RECORD GROUP IDEAS

2   BRAINSTORM A LIST OF OBSERVABLE EFFECTS THAT COULD BE INDICES OF ORGANIZATIONAL EFFICIENCY OR NON-EFFICIENCY AS A RESULT OF THIS TRAINING PROGRAMME

  EXAMPLES:
  – REPORT ERRORS
  – OPERATING COSTS
  – LOSSES
  – ABSENTEEISM RATE
  – SICK LEAVE ABUSE
  – COMPLAINTS
  – WRITTEN REPORTS LATE
  – ETC.

Figure 23   On-the-job training evaluation transparency 1

programme covered improving written communications.

3   After the brainstorming session, call time and use the transparency in Figure 24.

4   After the groups have reported their findings, pass out the handout shown in Figure 25. Ask the participants to individually read the instructions.

5   Use the transparency shown in Figure 26 to show the participants an example. (You may use your own example that fits the programme that you are presenting.)

6   Pass out the 'On-The-Job Evaluation Form' found in Figure 27. Ask the participants to individually select several of the specific observable effects that were presented, and write up their own real sets of data on the evaluation form. Tell them that they can select either their section/department/unit or a real individual employee – or both.

7   Give the participants time to complete at least one set of data. Then call time and obtain oral feedback from each participant on his or her set of data.

8   Indicate days that you will be available for a follow-up meeting in about four weeks' time. Circulate a sign-up sheet and ask each participant to select a day and time for a 30-minute meeting with you. The purpose of this meeting will be to review their evaluation form and obtain a copy of it in order to compile the potential cost savings for the

---

ON-THE-JOB TRAINING EVALUATION
(Continued)

3   AFTER YOUR BRAINSTORMING SESSION, SCREEN OUT AND DELETE THE FOLLOWING:

  – NON-APPLICABLE ITEMS
  – YOUR OWN BEHAVIOURS (YOU ARE OBSERVING NOT WHAT YOU DO, BUT THE EFFECTS OF WHAT YOU DO.)
  – ITEMS THAT CANNOT BE TRACKED

    EXAMPLES:
      – THE INFORMATION IS NOT AVAILABLE
      – THE BEHAVIOURS CANNOT BE OBSERVED

4   SELECT 5 OR 6 REAL ITEMS THAT YOUR GROUP CAN USE TO EVALUATE THE PROGRAMME

5   COST EACH OF THE ITEMS SELECTED IN TERMS OF POTENTIAL POUNDS SAVED OR LOST OVER A ONE-YEAR PERIOD

6   REPORT GROUP'S FINDINGS

Figure 24   On-the-job training evaluation transparency 2

ON-THE-JOB EVALUATION RECORD
OR, 'HOW DO WE KNOW THE TRAINING WORKS?'

This sheet and the accompanying form were designed by actual participants in an ITC workshop. They felt that today's training must be looked at in terms of return on investment. We heartily concur. In other words, if training is to be cost effective, then we must be able to show measurable results. This form should enable you to track measurable changes – and prove to yourself and others whether the time spent in training results in a sizeable return on investment.

EXAMPLES OF OBSERVABLE EFFECTS:

Down time
% of rejects
Returns
Report errors
Performance records
Operating costs

Number of reprimands
Losses
Number of days absent
Tardiness
Other employee complaints
Sick leave abuse

Doesn't have daily 'To Do' list
Leaves early
Desk or work area cluttered
Long lunch breaks
Written work late

WHEN USING THE EVALUATION FORM:

1. Select observable effects that fit your specific section, department or individual being tracked, and the training programmes being presented.
2. Analyse each effect, and determine what should be going on (standard, or target desired), and then what is actually going on (present actual deficiency). Note that most of the above examples of deficiencies are NOT specific enough to be used. Actual quality, quantity, cost and time numbers should be used.
3. Select only 3 to 5 key sets of observable effects for your department, section, unit or individual that you want to evaluate. Selecting too many effects will unduly complicate your tracking job. If possible, cost each of these in terms of dollars saved over a one-year time period.
4. Determine the specific time period you want to evaluate – i.e., 1 month, 3 months, 6 months, 1 year, etc. Next, determine the recording dates within that time period (i.e., daily, weekly, every other week, monthly, etc.). Then, write the dates horizontally across the form where indicated ['DATES (specific day … etc.)'].
5. During the evaluation period, you will then record actual figures, numbers, percentages or appropriate data in the horizontal 'numbers' rows, under the appropriate column.

EXAMPLE:

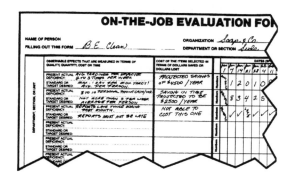

Figure 25   On-the-job training evaluation handout

PROBLEM EMPLOYEES	Name: Tom Swift	OBSERVABLE EFFECTS MEASURED IN TERMS OF QUALITY, QUANTITY, COST OR TIME		COST OF ITEMS SELECTED IN TERMS OF POUNDS SAVED OR LOST
		PRESENT ACTUAL DEFICIENCY	Employee has been tardy 5 times during past month. 2 Hours Lost Time/Mon. 2 Hours/Mon. Supervisory Time Spent on Problem	2 Hr. Lost Time × £20 Burden Rate = £40/Mon. £40 × 12 Mon. = £480
		STANDARD OR TARGET DESIRED	Employee is not expected to be tardy more than once per month. 1/5 Hour Lost Time 1/2 Hour Supervisory Time Spent on Follow-up	2 Hr. Supv. Time × £50 Burden Rate = £100/Mon £100 × 12 Mon. = £1200 £1200 + £480 = £1680 TOTAL

Figure 26   On-the-job training evaluation example transparency

entire group. At this time you can also schedule a six-month (or one-year) follow-up meeting to determine the real cost savings.

This is a remarkable process! It will not only give you a good idea of the cost savings resulting from your training programme, but you can also calculate the total cost of the training and thus arrive at a fairly accurate picture of your return on investment. In addition, by developing their own indices of measurement, the participants become committed to actually using the ideas learned in the programme – and measuring the results!

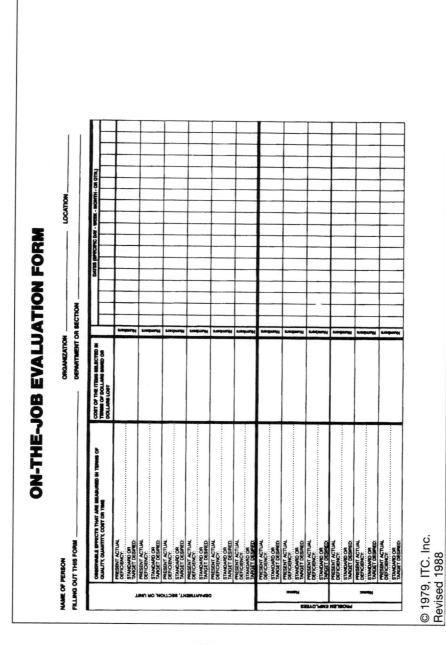

© 1979, ITC. Inc.
Revised 1988

Figure 27   On-the-job evaluation form

97

Off-the-shelf Packaged Programmes

Off-the-shelf packaged programmes

A few years ago, if the film you ordered (there weren't any videotapes) arrived with a single page of instructions for its use, you would consider yourself fortunate. Things have changed! In 1974, Dr Bill Byham, CEO of Development Dimensions International, released a series of ten one-half day behavioural modelling programmes, complete with videotapes, leader's guide and participant manuals. In 1977, International Training Consultants released its series of eight one-half day skill-building packages. Zenger Miller followed soon after with their training packages. Today almost all main suppliers are no longer in the film business, but instead offer full lines of training packages 'to go'. To date, thousands of pre-engineered packaged programmes have been sold to trainers all over the world who are very happy to allow someone else to do the work of research and development.

But having so many packaged programmes to choose from can make it difficult for you to decide the best programme for your needs. Therefore, in this section we will first discuss the factors that should be considered when making your selection, and then describe an effective process you can use to make your decisions.

Selection factors

There are six basic areas you need to consider when making packaged programme selection decisions: the programme's content; teaching processes; facilitator's aids; media; participant's aids; and the supplier. Even though not all of these factors may be important to you, we will review all six in detail because we each have different needs, and this will ensure that you do not inadvertently overlook a factor that might be important for you to consider when making your decision.

Content

I have listed content first because I believe it is the most important factor to consider. If the training content doesn't represent the majority of our participants' needs, then the rest doesn't matter – we shouldn't consider the programme in any case. Thus it is vital that a good planning process be used to ensure that you understand exactly what your participants need to know, before making a decision on a specific training package. (Step 1 through to 6 of the planning process described in this book is an example of what you might use to determine content.) If you don't take the time to analyse the content needs of your participants, then how are you going to be able to choose one programme over another? Packaged programmes ARE different. Some will work for you – and others won't!

When you feel reasonably certain of what your participants' needs are, the first step is to make sure that the packaged programme's objectives and detailed content outline match your needs. In addition, look for flexibility. Can you easily delete unwanted content presented in the packaged programmes, and/or add missing material? And most important, will the supplier of the material allow you to customize their programme in this way? If not, you might want to look at other programmes.

Process

The teaching process used in the training programme should match your own style, the participants' needs and your organization's needs. For example, if your style is to make presentations, you are going to require a lot of help! You will want videotapes that have good 'edutainment' value; and detailed participant's manuals so your participants will remember what you talked about. If your style is more participative, look for built-in subgroup workshops and opportunities for group discussions. Or if you are more 'laid back' and let your groups 'do their own thing', then you will need packaged programmes that have open-ended case work, low-structured exercises and plenty of games.

If your participants are more comfortable with a training style of 'sit back, shut up and listen to my lecture', then you may not be able to use processes that are totally unstructured. But usually our participants appreciate and enjoy group work that is participative – though presented and led with some structure.

When evaluating the available packaged programmes, look closely for variety in the way the programme is presented. Are the strategies varied, as well as the media used to teach the content? Is the programme broken up into clean, discrete elements? Do each of these elements give you an opportunity to: 1) obtain information from the participants, 2) present information to them, 3) help them assimilate the information presented, and, 4) have them apply the information in the classroom?

Last, has the supplier gone to the trouble to design a pre- and post-test for the programme? As we discussed earlier, testing can be a very effective way of involving the participants in the programme, as well as determining how well they learned the material.

Facilitator

Let's talk first about training suppliers that require that trainers who purchase their packages be 'certified' before they can facilitate the programme. Frankly, I feel that such a policy does more for the supplier's pocketbook than it does for the trainer's needs. To require a competent 20-year veteran trainer, for example, to be 'certified' before he or she can use the programme is, in my opinion, almost unethical! After all, don't we all (including suppliers) claim that we only do training when the organization needs a specific programme? Is this philosophy any different for the trainer who may not need the training that he or she is forced to take in order to use a particular supplier's programme?

My feeling is that certification is a *design* issue. In other words, it is the supplier's responsibility to develop and design material that most competent trainers will be able to use with their present level of training skills. Therefore, if 'Train-the-Trainer' programmes are offered by the supplier, they should be optional – not required! Some trainers, especially entry-level trainers, need additional help in being able to effectively present a packaged programme. But not all trainers need such assistance. And a 'certification' process will be particularly unnecessary if the packaged programme has been deliberately designed so that nearly all trainers can facilitate it.

If you have had some training experience and feel fairly comfortable leading your sessions, the chances are that you will do an outstanding job using a pre-engineered, packaged programme – if the programme is properly designed. Look at the leader's guide that is supplied with the programme? Does it give suggestions as to what you might say in presenting an exercise to your group? Are there places throughout the leader's guide where you can write in your own notes?

Does the packaged programme include not only 'content' transparencies, but also 'process' transparencies? As discussed earlier, process transparencies (which give group instructions) not only help the participants remember what they are supposed to do, but also make it much easier for you to facilitate the workshop.

Is everything that you will need in preparing for the workshop included in the leader's guide? For example, does the guide have a copy of the video script (so that you don't have to replay the videotape), as well as copies of the participant's worksheets, cases and assignments? (On the other hand, there can be too much of a good thing. I am embarrassed to remember that I once produced a two-day training module that had a 170-page leader's guide. Talk about overkill!)

Media

In this section, 'media' refers only to videotapes. At this point in our discussion, let us assume that the media content of a package closely matches your training needs. But we still need to ask the same kinds of questions that were presented on page 77, like:

- Is the setting appropriate for your organization?
- Does the videotape appear to be out of date?
- Are the actors believable?
- Is the script believable?
- How good is the technical quality of the production?

When you are evaluating a packaged programme, don't begin by playing the videotape. First examine the leader's guide to determine how the videotape should be used. Then play the videotape. I am speaking from experience. One of our best selling training modules is a one-day workshop on 'Time Management'. Built in is an unusual videotape that is to be played at the beginning of the workshop. The video shows a very 'nice guy' who gets into considerable trouble because he doesn't manage his time properly. This video presentation becomes the core of a powerful experiential learning exercise that helps the participants accept responsibility for controlling their own time. Yet, time after time trainers (who ought to know better) preview and return the videotape with the evaluation: 'Using a negative modelling tape will teach our people what to do wrong.' When contacted on follow-up, they confess that they didn't look at anything else in the package, and didn't know that the videotape was not a 'modelling' tape at all! So examine the whole package, and how the parts fit together. And look at the leader's guide *first* so that you know how each component is to be used.

Participants

First examine the participant's workbook. Is the writing style suitable for your participants? Does it read well? Are words and references used that can soon make the material appear obsolete? (I recently read a workbook that referred to a now-defunct football league.) Does the workbook adequately cover the programme's content, as well as provide worksheets for role plays and classroom exercises? Is it complete enough to offer back-on-the-job help for your participants?

And most important: Can you reproduce it? If you plan to train a number of people, then not only can the cost become prohibitive, but you may well lose budget control if the supplier increases your future price. Last, what other job aids are supplied (key step cards, cases, worksheets, etc.) – and can you reproduce those aids?

Supplier

What kind of history does this supplier have for service AFTER the sale – and how can you find out this information? Who else in your local area has used this training package? What other creditable organizations, or organizations like yours, have used this package and will the supplier furnish you with their names and phone numbers?

What is the supplier's policy toward such issues as mandatory 'certification', and copyright release on the participant's information? If several of your trainers are going to implement the training programme, will this supplier sell extra leader's guides, transparency sets and videotapes to meet your needs?

And last, what is the cost of the programme – considering not only the initial cost, but the eventual cost as well, if you are to be charged per person for extra participant's workbooks? In other words, are you getting value for money or are you being 'taken to the cleaners'?

Selection process

I have borrowed and modified Kepner-Tregoe's (KT) decision-making grid to help us in our selection process. You may recall that their process consists of four basic steps: 1) write a decision statement; 2) develop your objectives; 3) create alternatives; and, 4) evaluate risk.

In most cases, your decision statement is straightforward – at least it should be! If you haven't conducted a needs assessment and carefully identified the specific things you want to teach your participants, then you are not prepared to purchase a packaged programme. But if you did your homework and you know exactly what specific content you want to teach (e.g., using steps 1–6 in the foregoing planning process), then the decision statement is considerably easier.

For example, suppose that you conducted a needs assessment and found that there was an urgent need for a quality programme on conducting performance appraisal interviews. Since you didn't have time to develop your own material from scratch, you made the decision to purchase a pre-packaged programme. But before you picked up the phone and called your favourite training material supplier, you took the time to determine the behaviours that needed to be taught, verified those behaviours by conducting interviews with a sample of the target population and then wrote your training objectives. Now you are ready for step one – writing a decision statement.

1   DECISION STATEMENT:

   'Select the best performance appraisal training package for our needs.'

2   SELECTION FACTORS
Step two is to now list all the factors (KT calls them 'objectives') that we should consider when we later evaluate the available alternatives. Then, since some of the factors are more important than others, weigh each factor on a scale of 1 (least important) to 10 (most important). Some of the factors and their weights might be:

Factors	Weight
A Number of our major training objectives covered by the packaged programme	10
B Initial cost	5
C Supplier train-the-trainer	7

	'certification' required even for experienced trainers	
D	Train-the-trainer programme available if needed	1
E	Supplier support (after the sale)	3
F	Reputation in the HRD community	4
G	Multi-media	9
H	Ease of use	7
I	Cost of additional participant's booklets or manuals	8
J	Release date of videotape	5
K	Ability of participants to relate to scenes in videotape	8
L	Available within four weeks	9
M	Can purchase only the programme needed (don't have to buy a minimum number of modules)	10
N	Vender visibility (Are participants subjected to commercials in the material?)	6

At this point we have listed the selection factors that are important to us. Note that this list, and the assigned weights, would be different for different trainers. In our hypothetical example, 'Available within four weeks' is important since the programme is scheduled to start in six weeks (thus we gave it a '9').

3   The next step in our analysis is to determine what alternatives are available. When you determine alternatives, seek help! Talk to other people whose opinions you respect and trust – *especially* if their opinions are likely to differ from yours. Then brainstorm a list of alternatives. Finally, select the best alternatives for evaluation.

Let us suppose that we have decided to evaluate suppliers 'X', 'Y' and 'Z'. From advertisements, brochures and our own knowledge of the available programmes, we should be able to obtain some of the required information. In other cases, we may have to do some 'networking', and call our friends at other organizations who are using packaged programmes. Note that as much as possible we write in INFORMATION: facts and figures, not 'yes/no', or vague ratings like 'good/better/best'. If an alternative is 'best', it's best for a reason. Write down the REASON, not the rating.

Factors	Weight	Alternatives		
		X	Y	Z
A Number of our main training objectives covered by the packaged programme	10	9 of 11	6 of 11	8 of 11
B Initial cost	5	£995	£875	£950
C Supplier train-the-trainer 'certification' required even for experienced trainers	7	No	Yes	Yes
D Train-the-trainer programme available if needed	1	Yes	Yes	Yes
E Supplier support (after the sale)	3	Only by phone	Local rep.	300 miles from supplier
F Reputation in the HRD community	4	Excellent	Excellent	Excellent
G Multi-media	9	Video & 40 transparencies	Video & two audio tapes	Video
H Ease of use	7	63-page Leader's Guide	31-page Leader's Guide	Very short Leader's Guide
I Cost of additional participant's booklets or manuals	8	N/C, print our own	£50	£45
J Release date of videotape	5	1986	1985	1983 (long hair)
K Ability of participants to relate to scenes in videotape	8	Gen. office	Sales Mgr.	Gen. office
L Available within four weeks	9	Yes	Yes	Yes
M Can purchase only the programme needed (don't have to buy a minimum number of modules)	10	Yes	Yes	Yes
N Vender visibility (Are participants subjected to commercials in the material?)	6	No	No	No

4   We then weigh and compare the ALTERNATIVES with each other using a 1-to-10 scale. Note that a '10' is automatically assigned to the best alternative and numbers below '10' to the others. (This will keep us from 'double-weighting' an objective.) We then multiply the factor weight by the alternative weight. Last, add up the multiplied figures for each alternative and see which is the highest scoring alternative.

Factors	Weight	Alternatives		
		X	Y	Z
A Number of our main training objectives covered by the packaged programme	10	9 of 11 (10 = 100)	6 of 11 (5) = 50	8 of 11 (8) = 80
B Initial cost	5	£995 (5) = 25	£875 (10) = 50	£950 (7) = 35
C Supplier train-the-trainer 'certification' required even for experienced trainers	7	No (10) = 70	Yes (0) = 0	Yes (0) = 0
D Train-the-trainer programme available if needed	1	Yes (10) = 10	Yes (10) = 10	Yes (10) = 10
E Supplier support (after the sale)	3	Only by phone (3) = 9	Local rep. (10) = 30	300 miles (5) = 15
F Reputation in the HRD community	4	Excellent (10) = 40	Excellent (10) = 40	Excellent (10) = 40
G Multi-media	9	Video & 40 transparencies (10) = 90	Video & two audio tapes (5) = 45)	Video (3) = 27
H Ease of use	7	63-page Leader's Guide (10) = 70	31-page Leader's Guide (7) = 49	Very short Leader's Guide (2) = 14
I Cost of additional participant's booklets or manuals	8	N/C, print our own (10) = 80	£50 (3) = 24	£45 (2) = 16
J Release date of videotape	5	1986 (10) = 50	1985 (9) = 45	1983 (long hair) (1) = 5
K Ability of participants to relate to scenes in videotape	8	Gen. office (10) = 80	Sales Mgr. (5) = 40	Gen. office (10) = 80
L Available within four weeks	9	Yes (10) = 90	Yes (10) = 90	Yes (10) = 90
M Can purchase only the programme needed, (don't have to buy a minimum number of modules)	10	Yes (10) = 100	Yes (10) = 100	Yes (10) = 100
N Vender visibility (Are participants subjected to commercials in the material?)	6	No (10) = 60	No (10) = 60	No (10) = 60
Totals		874	633	572

Note that there were several factors that had identical information for each of the alternatives. Since the scores are therefore identical for each of these factors and related alternatives, you may choose not to include them in the list of added scores if you are only interested in the ranking of the alternative suppliers (1st, 2nd, etc.).

5   In our last step, we carefully analyse the RISK (R) involved in making our decision. We do this by evaluating the potential risk that could occur if we selected either of our top two alternatives. (If the total scores of all of the alternatives are close, then evaluate the risk with all of them.)

To determine the risk involved in an alternative, simply ask, 'If I do this, what can go wrong?' Once again, seek out help from others with experience, since several individuals can foresee future problems that one person may overlook. When first considering potential risks, deal with one alternative at a time; do not attempt initially to evaluate the possibility of each risk occurring in other alternatives.

When you have a full list of potential problems for the first alternative, only then should you evaluate each potential problem in terms of the PROBABILITY (P) of its happening, and its SERIOUSNESS (S) if it does happen. Again, use a scale of 1–10 to assign probability and seriousness weights to each of your risks. Multiply the two weights, add up the numbers, and the resultant score will give some indication of the amount of risk involved in that particular alternative. Then, using the same procedure, evaluate other alternatives as needed.

A final point: don't 'double-load' a risk. If 'Ease of use' is a listed factor, then don't rewrite it as a risk, 'Difficult to use'. And if you end up with a risk that is common to all the alternatives, then you probably missed a factor in your original list.

Alternative 1 X		Alternative 2 Y	
Potential problems	$P \times S = R$	Potential problems	$P \times S = R$
They are a small company. What if they go out of business?	$1 \times 5 = 5$	Since they are going to charge us for future participant's booklets, they could control our future budgets.	$8 \times 2 = 16$

Compare the original alternative scores from step 3 with the risk scores from step 4, and make a balanced decision. Do not subtract the risk score from the alternative score – they are different things. In our example, alternative 'X', with a score of 874 and a risk of only 5, is easily the best choice.

In using this process, ask for help! Form a committee of five or so concerned individuals. You might ask one or two of the key future participants in the programme, a member of management, a respected member of your staff or even an outside HRD specialist from another organization, to be on the advisory committee. Prior to calling the meeting, make sure you have clearly determined what the specific programme objectives are, and have also obtained brochures, catalogues, flyers and previews of the actual training material from the suppliers of the packaged programmes. Then call the meeting; and use a flip chart to make the decision process visible for your committee. The following is a summary of this step-by-step process:

1   Write out your decision statement at the top of the first sheet of flip chart paper. Then brainstorm and list under it the factors that need to be considered.
2   Next, discuss and combine the factors, writing them more formally on a second sheet of flip chart paper, with the decision statement also rewritten at the top (leave some room for the alternatives to be added later). Then weigh the final factors using a 1–10 scale.
3   Evaluate the packaged programmes that are available, select the best three or four and write these alternatives at the top of the flip chart paper.
4   Write on the grid the information needed; and then compare and weigh each alternative factor's information, giving the best package an automatic '10'.
5   Multiply the factor weight by the alternative weight and add the resultant scores.
6   On a third sheet of flip chart paper, select the best two alternatives and evaluate each – one at a time – for potential problems. For each potential problem, determine the probability of the event occurring and the seriousness of the event if it does.
7   Compare the alternative total scores with the risk scores, and make a balanced decision. (Again, do not subtract risk scores from the alternative scores.) Last, after making a decision, see if your committee can find any way to reduce the risk of the potential problems that may have surfaced for the alternative that was selected. Discuss with the committee how you might reduce the probability of the problem occurring in the first place. Or if it occurs regardless, how can the potential problem's impact be reduced?

This decision process isn't guaranteed to avoid every problem. But it helps greatly to arrive at an intelligent and sound selection. What you do is important, and it is worth spending extra time to ensure that whatever training package you buy is right for you, your participants and your organization.

Using Outside Training Consultants

Using outside training consultants

There are some good reasons for deciding to choose an outside consultant to facilitate a training programme for your organization. One was taught to me by Jay Beacroft, my boss at 3M, some 15 years ago. Jay said, 'To be a good trainer doesn't mean you always have to BE the resource. It means you have to MANAGE your resources!'

The following are some of the common-sense reasons why you might elect to hire an outside consultant – and 'manage' your resources:

1 If your executives need a workshop on a particular topic, and some of the people in this group remember when you worked in the mail room, you may have a 'credibility' problem. In this case, you might decide to bring in an outside consultant to administer the programme.
2 You may find you will need outside help if the topic is totally unfamiliar to you, and you don't have the time to do the necessary research in order to determine the content or design the programme.
3 Or, you may not be able to justify investing the significant amount of time required to design a one-time, specialized programme for a limited number of participants.
4 Last, your organization may need a significant training effort (e.g., training all first-line supervisors) and it is simply impossible for you to do it all yourself. In such a case, it may be much more effective to hire an outside consultant.

Here, keep in mind that if all you need is a generic 'Time Management' programme, almost any consultant can do it for a reasonable cost. But if what you want is a programme that meets highly specific needs within your organization, a consultant will need to spend significant time to develop the programme – and be prepared for a large budgetary item!

Consultants are, in effect, selling their 'body' for time. And there is only a limited amount of time to sell. Thus the principle of supply and demand will require you to pay a large fee for qualified consultants. Good consultants stay busy – as busy as they want to be – and will charge considerably more for their time. But there is also a question of experience. The more experience the consultant has had with your particular training need, the less up-front preparation and development may be required. So it is a trade-off. More experienced consultants will charge more per day, but may require less time to deliver what you need.

Unfortunately, there is a heavy turnover of available consultants. It is an easy business to get into (if you are fired, you can call yourself a 'consultant' until you get hired again) but a tough business to stay in. Look in the yellow pages of your local phone book under the heading 'Consultants'. Then, compare this list with the list found in a five-year-old phone book. The odds are that less than 20 per cent of the names will be the same. But also, the chances are that the consultants who have been around for a number of years are outstanding; they must be to survive. Thus, one of the key things to look for when selecting a consultant is experience.

Making the decision

When you need to select a consultant, you can use the same KT decision-making process earlier in the section on packaged programmes. Let's look now at factors that you need to consider in selecting a consultant for your organization's training needs:

1 **Experience with the training content that will be taught**
   As already mentioned, the more experience the consultant has had with the training topic in question, the quicker he or she will be able to respond to your organization's needs. One of the things you are buying when you hire a consultant is his or her experience. You don't want to pay – any more than you have to – for the consultant's own training.

   For example, if you plan to conduct 'Quality Circle' training for your people, then you really need someone who has had particular experience in this area. Ask your prospective consultant for samples of his or her work from past jobs of a similar nature to yours – handouts that the consultant designed, programme outlines and objectives or exercises used. Good consultants also get published in the leading training magazines. Ask to see copies of published articles, especially ones that relate to the content that will be taught at your organization. Last, let the consultant know in your initial meeting that you must review and approve all written material that will be passed out in the training session.

2 **Experience with your type of organization**
The more experience the consultant has had with organizations like yours, the easier it will be to develop and deliver a programme for you. In addition, the consultant will have more credibility with your group if he or she has had experience with similar groups in other organizations. If you are in a financial business, you may prefer to select a consultant that has had experience in this area. Similarly, health care organizations may choose someone with a hospital background; and educational institutions may need a consultant who has had experience in education. Most consultants have specialities, not only in the services they offer, but also in terms of the markets they service.

3 **Experience with the type of individuals who will be participants in the programme**
If your plans are to conduct an executive retreat, you should find a consultant who has had ample experience with executives. Or if you plan to do first-line supervisor training, you will need a consultant who can 'talk their language'. The same is true for sales and marketing. It is very difficult for an outside consultant who has never had real sales experience to conduct a sales training programme for a group of high-volume salespeople.

4 **Availability of the consultant**
The better the consultant is, the longer lead time he or she will need. Good consultants are booked up months in advance. Therefore, the earlier you can do your planning, the better selection you will have in terms of available consultants.

5 **Quality of the consultant's work**
When you hire a consultant, you are putting your reputation on the line with your organization. When a good consultant finishes your job, you can be a hero. But a bad one is trouble! So do some networking with your professional associates. And when you make the appointment for the initial interview, ask your prospective consultant to bring references and evaluations from the last three workshops he or she conducted. Then check them out. Unfortunately, most consultants have large stacks of 'happiness' evaluations which they collected at the end of especially good workshops. So don't settle for those. Call the references from the last three consecutive workshops conducted by the consultant and ask for their candid evaluation of the job done.

6   **Cost**

If I could give you a piece of advice here, it is: Don't haggle! I once read an article written by an individual who described his delight in beating down the consultant's price. He then had the audacity to suggest that a consultant will respect the trainer who does this. In my opinion this trainer (with a very large US corporation) was projecting his value system on to others, and rather than gaining respect, likely lost it – both for himself and for his organization. As you interview various consultants and network with your peers at other organizations, you can rather quickly determine the going rate for quality consultants in your area.

Working with a consultant

When you make a decision to use a particular training consultant, your responsibilities are not over. These may include:

- Help the consultant to learn the 'language' of the organization.
- Share all of your background information on the training project, including its history, the planning you have already done and any ideas about special problems the consultant may encounter.
- If you commit to a specific date for a training programme, don't call at the last minute and cancel. This type of action speaks loudly about your planning abilities and the effectiveness of your organization.
- Furnish the training consultant with a brief biography of each of the participants who will be in the training programme(s). This will help the consultant learn about the people, and their names, prior to the session. Nothing impresses participants more than to be welcomed by name by an outside consultant on the first day of a training programme.
- Obtain a biography from the consultant and provide each participant with it before the session.
- Pay promptly. Consultants are concerned about cash flow. It simply isn't fair to your consultant to pay him or her months after the job is over because you 'forgot' to process the paperwork.
- Ask the consultant to conduct a pilot programme before doing wall-to-wall training. This will give you time to determine if the consultant is really right for your organization, as well as giving the consultant time to modify any part of the programme that needs changing.
- When the pilot programme is conducted, it is your clear responsibility to, 1) prepare and deliver a thorough introduction of the consultant to

the participants; and, 2) be present in the room the entire day. A trainer who pops in and out of a classroom throughout the day communicates to the participants, by his or her actions, a low estimate of the importance of the programme.

Finally, avoid formal 'contracts' if possible. Letters of intent from you to the consultant and vice versa work quite well, and are much less bothersome. On a personal note, in my years of working as a consultant, most of the formal proposals I saw I did not feel were worth bidding on. They included pages upon pages of detail (especially in government proposals), so that to read and respond appropriately was not worth the time required. Possibly it is my southern heritage; but I operated as a consultant for 15 years with only a handshake. In all that time, I only signed one contract, and that was in my first year of business – when I didn't know better.

Appendix: Programme Development Forms

Appendix: Programme development forms

The forms provided on the following pages may be copied and used in designing your own programmes. These forms include:

Page 1 – Behaviour Worksheet (Step 1)
Page 2 – Undesirable Behaviours Worksheet (Step 2)
Page 3 – Final List of Behaviours Worksheet (Steps 3 and 4)
Page 4 – Training Objectives Worksheet (Step 5)
Page 5 – Programme Development Worksheet – Putting It All Together (Steps 6, 7, 8 and 9)

Examples of typical evaluation worksheets (Step 10) have been included in the evaluation section (pages 95 and 97).

PROGRAMME TITLE: _____

REFERENCES: TITLE OF BOOK OR ARTICLE   **AUTHOR**

_____
_____
_____
_____
_____
_____
_____
_____

1   POSITIVE BEHAVIOURS (not necessarily in a special order at this time):

_____
_____
_____
_____
_____
_____
_____
_____
_____
_____
_____
_____
_____
_____
_____
_____
_____
_____
_____
_____
_____

Reproduced from *Designing Training Programmes* by Dick Leatherman, Gower, Aldershot

2 A   IDENTIFY UNDESIRABLE PARTICIPANT BEHAVIOURS (If the behaviour is already written as a positive behaviour on page 1, do not rewrite it as a negative behaviour on this page.)

_____
_____
_____
_____
_____
_____
_____
_____
_____
_____
_____
_____
_____
_____
_____
_____
_____
_____
_____

B   REWRITE UNDESIRABLE BEHAVIOURS IN POSITIVE FORM

_____
_____
_____
_____
_____
_____
_____
_____
_____
_____
_____
_____
_____
_____

3 FINAL LIST OF ALL BEHAVIOURS (in the order in which they naturally occur in the task, with negative behaviours included in positive form):

4 VERIFICATION OF BEHAVIOURS BY INTERVIEWS (needed = 'Yes'; not needed = 'No')

5 TRAINING OBJECTIVES WORKSHEET. (Write objectives on only those behaviours that the participants need to learn.)

Objective: A description of the participants' desired behaviours when they have successfully completed a learning experience.

            – OBSERVABLE behaviours   – MEASURABLE behaviours

A   Identify specific behaviours that need to be taught.
B   Make the objectives quantifiable if possible.
C   Write objectives that are achievable.

PROGRAMME DEVELOPMENT WORKSHEETS

OBJECTIVE

ASK

ADVISE	

ASSIMILATE

APPLY

Reproduced from *Designing Training Programmes* by Dick Leatherman, Gower, Aldershot

Recommended reading

Barca, Michèle and Cobb, Kate (1993), *Beginnings and Endings*, Aldershot: Gower.

Bourner, Tom, Martin, Vivien and Race, Phil (1993), *Workshops that Work*, Maidenhead: McGraw-Hill.

Buckley, Roger and Caple, Jim (1990), *The Theory and Practice of Training*, London: Kogan Page.

Caffarella, Rosemary S. (1988), *Program Development and Evaluation Resource Book for Trainers*, New York: John Wiley & Sons.

Corder, Colin (1990), *Teaching Hard, Teaching Soft*, Aldershot: Gower.

Craig, Robert L. (1987), *Training and Development Handbook (ASTD, 3rd Edition)*, New York: McGraw-Hill.

Custer, Gene E. (1986), *Planning, Packaging, and Presenting Training*, San Diego: University Associates.

Davies, I. K. (1981), *Instructional Technique*, Maidenhead: McGraw-Hill.

Davis, John (1992), *How to Write a Training Manual*, Aldershot: Gower.

Forsyth, Patrick (1992), *Running an Effective Training Session*, Aldershot: Gower.

Honey, Peter and Mumford, Alan (1982), *Manual of Learning Styles*, Maidenhead: Honey.

Jones, Ken (1988), *Interactive Learning Events: A Guide for Facilitators*, London: Kogan Page.

Mager, Robert F. (1984), *Preparing Instructional Objectives*, London: Pitman.

Mayo, Douglas G. and DuBois, Philip H. (1987), *The Complete Book of*

Training: Theory, Principles, and Techniques, San Diego: University Associates.

Nadler, Leonard (1982), *Designing Training Programs: The Critical Events Model*, Reading, MA: Addison-Wesley.

Newby, A. C. (1992), *Training Evaluation Handbook*, Aldershot: Gower.

Odiorne, George S. (1970), *Training by Objectives: An Economic Approach to Management Training*, New York: The Macmillan Company.

Pont, Tony (1991), *Developing Effective Training Skills*, Maidenhead: McGraw-Hill.

Prior, John (ed.) (1994), *Gower Handbook of Training and Development*, 2nd edition, Aldershot: Gower.

Rae, Leslie (1995), *Techniques of Training*, 3rd edition, Aldershot: Gower.

Tracey, William R. (1985), *Training for Results: A Systems Approach to the Development of Human Resources in Industry*, New York: AMACOM.

Index